Real Life Financial Planning for Physicians

A Physician's Guide to Financial Security

Todd D. Bramson, CFP®, ChFC, CLU
Jon C. Ylinen

ASPATORE

©2012 Thomson Reuters/Aspatore
All rights reserved. Printed in the United States of America.

No part of this publication may be reproduced or distributed in any form or by any means, or stored in a database or retrieval system, except as permitted under Sections 107 or 108 of the U.S. Copyright Act, without prior written permission of the publisher. This book is printed on acid-free paper.

Material in this book is for educational purposes only. This book is sold with the understanding that neither any of the authors nor the publisher is engaged in rendering legal, accounting, investment, or any other professional service as a part of this book. Neither the publisher nor the authors assume any liability for any errors or omissions or for how this book or its contents are used or interpreted or for any consequences resulting directly or indirectly from the use of this book. For legal advice or any other, please consult your personal lawyer or the appropriate professional.

The views expressed by the individuals in this book (or the individuals on the cover) do not necessarily reflect the views shared by the companies they are employed by (or the companies mentioned in this book). The employment status and affiliations of authors with the companies referenced are subject to change.

For additional copies or customer service inquiries, please e-mail west.customer.service@thomson.com.

ISBN 978-0-314-28237-8

Mat #41305098

Dedications

This book is dedicated to our clients, business partners and staff, and especially, our families……without whom, we wouldn't have learned the most important lesson of life…which is: "When all is said and done, it is the quality and depth of relationships and experiences that are the essence of life…not the accumulation of material possessions."

Todd D. Bramson and Jon C. Ylinen

Thank You

We extend a special thank you to…
…our clients, who have trusted us with their financial decisions.
…our staff, partners, and business associates, who make work a pleasure.
…attorney Robert Kaufer for his valuable contribution to this book. Bob's insight and knowledge and his ability to communicate this effectively are evident in the estate planning and asset protection chapter, which he wrote.

Lastly, a special thank you from Todd to Mishelle Shepard, who kept encouraging and helping me throughout the process of writing the first book, *Real Life Financial Planning*. Who would have known that the original idea would have blossomed into a successful book series?

Real Life Financial Planning for Physicians

Contents

	Preface	7
1	Getting Started	9
2	Where Do I Start?	15
3	The Pyramid	23
4	The Security and Confidence Stage	27
5	Disability Income Insurance	35
6	Life Insurance	41
7	The Capital Accumulation Stage	49
8	The Tax-Advantaged Stage	61
9	529 College Savings Plans	75
10	The Speculation Stage	81
11	Estate Planning with Asset Protection Strategies	83
12	Case Studies	95
	Appendix A: Employee Benefits Checklist	121
	About the Authors	127

Preface

With over thirty-two years of combined experience, we have had the privilege of building a unique and specialized financial planning practice catering almost exclusively to physicians. When asked, "What do you do?" the answer is, on the surface, pretty simple. We work with residents, fellows, and staff and in practice physicians, helping them clearly identify their financial goals and objectives, and then work to develop a very comprehensive, structured, and coordinated financial plan. We then monitor, review and update the plan regularly.

However, when you consider the myriad of financial decisions and the ramifications these decisions can have on you and your family, it is easy to understand that building and maintaining a sound financial plan is a never-ending and complicated process. As the world becomes more sophisticated and information becomes so accessible, you would assume making sound financial decisions would be easier than in years past, not more difficult. Remember......access to information does not mean access to wisdom.

With the bombardment of information, opinions, and advice coming from every angle, it becomes nearly impossible to make the time necessary to fully understand the various financial tools and strategies well enough to make sound decisions. Few occupations require as much time, education, and training as that of a physician. The dedication and commitment required to provide the highest quality care and stay on top of the ever-advancing field of medicine leaves little time for contemplation of financial decisions.

It is with this understanding that we decided to put our thoughts and experience on paper in an easy-to-read format. In fact, our clients are the ones who suggested we write this book as they mentioned to us how these concepts helped them finally understand how to organize and prioritize their financial decisions. Hopefully, this book will help make some sense of the complex world of financial planning. We hope you find this resource very helpful.

Todd D. Bramson and Jon C. Ylinen

Tax Disclosure

This information is a general discussion of the relevant federal tax laws. It is not intended for, nor can it be used by any taxpayer for the purpose of avoiding federal tax penalties. This information is provided to support the promotion or marketing of ideas that my benefit a taxpayer. Taxpayers should seek the advice of their own tax and legal advisors regarding any tax and legal issues applicable to their specific circumstances.

1

Getting Started

Why the title *Real Life Financial Planning for Physicians?*

We have spent over thirty-two combined years working directly with physician on their financial plans and financial planning questions. It often seems that most financial planning books or publications are written for the average person. Certainly, physicians will have some unique needs that need the help of a specialist. Hopefully, this book summarizes the wisdom we have learned and shared with our clients in individual meetings throughout the years. *Real Life Financial Planning Physicians* is simply a practical method of understanding, organizing, and prioritizing financial decisions.

Most financial planning publications and financial plans themselves assume that everyone lives a long, healthy life and saves a good portion of their income in quality investments that always do well. This book addresses all of the issues that happen in real life, and we hope you take the time to read this and work with a trained professional to develop a financial plan that meets *your* goals and objectives.

Why is there is an ever-increasing number of financial planning books on the market today?

Because there is an ever-increasing need to get educated.

- Few parents openly discuss financial matters with their children while they're growing up.
- Personal financial planning is rarely a subject taught in school. Most physicians have spent almost 20,000 hours educating

themselves on their specialty and not more than five to ten for personal financial planning, if that!
- Most physicians today begin their professional life already *in the red*. The average physician finishes their training with over $170,000 in debt. (And in some cases, much more!)
- Physicians live high-pressure, busy lifestyles that do not allow much free time to try and learn about all of the options they have.

These facts mean there are far too many medical specialists today who are ill-equipped to deal with the practical and fundamental necessities of planning for a secure and independent financial life.

Times have changed. Today more than ever, your financial future needs you. Long gone are the days when you could rely on your employer to pay back decades of loyal service with a comfortable pension plan. Certainly, the government can't assure you of a reasonable retirement after a lifetime of social security contributions. Not to mention the fact that financial issues have become increasingly complex and we are continually inundated with confusing financial information.

These facts aren't meant to cause stress, but rather to wake you up to the financial reality that thoughtful planning is needed immediately to help you balance and juggle all of the financial decisions you face. You must take control of your decisions and begin to educate yourself and take steps to using your education and training to set you up for a successful financial life.

Don't wait another day. This book is meant to give you an introduction into the often intimidating world of financial planning. You will learn about the variety of investments and insurance options. You will learn the lingo and get practical, "real-life" advice on where to go to next, whether you intend to go the road alone or get some help along the way. Best of all, you will gain ideas to help you climb the pyramid of financial success.

Financial success isn't, as most people might suspect, the ability to make one or two decisions that turn a dollar into a million. Rather, financial success is the result of many, many small but sound decisions that, when compounded, add up to substantial financial security.

Getting Started

You are in complete control. Or at least you should be. When it comes to spending and saving, investing and paying taxes, many may offer good advice, but you're the only one who can do anything about it. Maybe you're a chronic shopper. Maybe you're unsure of your investment options and how to prioritize them. Maybe you don't have a clue where your paycheck goes each month. In any case, if you're reading this book you already understand the importance of getting your future under control, and that's the crucial first step to financial freedom.

Who Needs a Financial Planner?

Financial independence and the accumulation of wealth are no accident. Granted, it's not possible to plan for every single event in life, but even tragedy can feel more manageable when you are financially prepared for it. *If you're like many people, you probably spend more time planning for a vacation than for your entire financial future!* Whether it's preparing for the future, securing yourself and your family against tragedy, or planning for the good times, your money deserves your undivided attention.

The truth is we all need to plan for our financial futures. So, the question is not whether to plan, but how to go about making a plan and whether we need a professional to help. The *information age* has intensified the field of financial planning. It is interesting to consider that thirty years ago financial news may have made top headlines two or three times throughout the year when the stock market would do particularly poorly or well, or if there was some other major economic news. Today, however, we have news programs dedicated to nothing else twenty-four/seven, and the number of financial headlines in the daily papers can be overwhelming. Still, there is a big difference between information and wisdom, and that's where the insight of a trusted professional can help.

These are the situations that may call for a financial planner's expertise:

- *You simply have no spare time.* If you're working for a large clinic or hospital, they may provide the groundwork for investing wisely for the long term, but even the best can't take into consideration the special circumstances of each individual or family. In this case, a financial planner can save you a bit of your most precious commodity—time.

- *You are easily bored or overwhelmed by financial questions.* If, for example, preparing a budget is such a nuisance that you can't even imagine having to sort through anything more complex, like insurance options, trends in mutual funds, or the stock market, then hiring a financial planner may be money well spent for greater financial confidence.

- *You are considering a complicated set of employee benefits in combination with personally owned insurance and investments.* You certainly don't want a new employer (or an existing employer who has changed their benefit structure) to conflict or overlap with your current investments. Such gaps or possible duplications should be examined thoroughly.

- *You are recently divorced or have lost a spouse who had previously been the one handling financial affairs for the household.* As if dealing with the trauma of divorce or death is not enough, being thrown into unknown financial waters without a trusted advisor can make you feel you're trying to stay afloat with bricks chained to your ankles.

- *You have recently finished your residency or fellowship and are suddenly thrust into making many important and critical decisions.* The saying "An ounce of prevention beats a pound of cure" is an important one in the world of financial planning. Seemingly insurmountable debt plagues the future of many physicians and surgeons. Learning to budget properly, to choose from insurance options, and to make wise investments are necessary life skills. Getting professional advice now beats paying for costly mistakes later.

- *You are running or will be starting your own private practice.* In this case, you most likely have to "wear many hats" as an entrepreneur. You are in sales, accounting, customer servicing, personnel, and oh yeah…practicing medicine, and probably don't have time to investigate or be aware of the many planning options available for you and your employees. A financial planner can help you sort through the many issues facing you.

As much as some of us would like to leave it all up to a professional, it's crucial that you understand the basics. A financial advisor is someone to

Getting Started

educate and advise you and assist you in taking action to develop a plan, but ultimately the final decisions are yours. A good financial planner will educate you as to the options you face, acting as a teacher, so that you understand all of the relevant issues. Then you can work together to create a plan and monitor it over the years. A successful financial plan is an ongoing process that stays up to date with your situation.

The topic doesn't matter...religion, politics, stocks, insurance, sales loads, or how to finance your house, just to name a few situations where there are many opinions. There are many individual considerations, and the correct solution depends on a variety of factors. We get leery of advice that suggests you should "always" do this or "never" do that. We believe that most financial decisions are far grayer than they are black and white.

We are not the first to say this, and we certainly won't be the last: *"It is crucial to trust your own judgment and instincts before taking action, no matter how good someone makes their argument."* The best way to gain confidence in your own better judgment is to educate yourself on the topic at hand.

With that in mind, in this book, you'll find answers to the most important financial questions facing everyone:

- How much money should I have in emergency reserves?
- In which order should I go about paying off my debts?
- Which is the right kind of insurance for me, and how much do I need?
- What are the most common financial mistakes people make?

You'll find the answers to these and many more of your questions as you read on.

2

Where Do I Start?

Your Net Worth Statement

The starting point of any financial plan is to figure out your current net worth. This is a snapshot of what you are worth at an exact point in time. In order to determine your net worth, you simply add up all of your assets and subtract all of your liabilities (debts). Often, when you are finishing your residency or fellowship training, your net worth is actually a negative number because the liabilities exceed the assets.

In order to measure your financial progress, it is important to know your net worth. Many people measure their financial progress by how much money they have in the bank. In reality, as the value of your assets go up, such as a house, business, or investments, and as you pay debts down, your net worth may be increasing more dramatically than you think. The most important way to measure financial progress is to calculate your net worth regularly. We use this to monitor your progress and spot trends just like you would watch a patient's cholesterol, blood pressure, or some other method of monitoring their health.

In simple terms, what would you be worth if you sold everything you owned and turned it into cash, and then paid off all your debts? If this is the first time you're preparing a net worth statement, it's also a good idea to try and estimate what you think your net worth has been over the last few years. Hopefully, you will be pleasantly surprised at the progress you've made.

There are several categories within the net worth statement.

Fixed assets are the first category. Fixed assets are those assets that have a relatively low risk of a loss of principal, or are backed by the government's or a financial institution's claims paying ability. Don't confuse this with fixed income investments (bonds), as those actually belong in the variable asset category. Fixed assets include the most conservative assets you have. A few examples would be checking and savings accounts, money market funds, certificates of deposit, T-bills, EE savings bonds, and whole life insurance cash values. These would be assets you have access to in an emergency; they are available any time, which means they are considered liquid.

Variable assets include most other financial assets. Examples include stocks, bonds, mutual funds, real estate investment trusts, retirement plans, or any investment where the principal can fluctuate.

Your personal and other assets would include tangible assets such as your house, personal, or business property, and vehicles. Other tangible assets such as a stereo, computer, or camera would also be included here.

Don't get too bogged down trying to establish a value for every piece of personal property. You may already have that information available from your homeowner's or renter's insurance policies, but if not, a rough estimate will work just fine. The main reason for gathering this information is to have an estimate so you can monitor trends.

*Tip: Use a phone or video camera to record each room in your house, including closets and the garage. In the event of a loss, it will be much easier to remember for the insurance company's reporting purposes.

Refer to the example of a very basic net worth statement for a young physician on the next page.

Fixed Assets:
- Savings Account — $5,000
- Checking Account — $3,000
- Certificate of Deposit — $2,000
- **Total Fixed Assets:** **$10,000**

Variable Assets:
- IRA — $3,000
- Mutual Funds — $5,000
- Individual Stocks — $2,000
- Variable Life Cash Value — $4,000
- 403b Balance — $20,000
- **Total Variable Assets:** **$34,000**

Personal and Other Assets:
- Condo — $200,000
- Vehicle — $20,000
- Personal Property — $20,000
- **Total Personal and Other:** **$240,000**

Total Assets: **$284,000**

Liabilities:
- Mortgage — $190,000
- Home Equity Line of Credit — $5,000
- Vehicle Loan — $10,000
- Student Loans — $140,000
- **Total Liabilities:** **$345,000**

Net Worth: Assets Minus Liabilities **-$61,000**

This way, when you are reviewing your net worth after some time, you will be able to track how this category has changed or to account for some of the money you spent.

For your liabilities, list the amount you owe if you could pay off the amount today, not the total of the payments over time, which would include interest. Subtract your total liabilities from your assets to arrive at your net worth. If you're like many people, this can be a sobering experience. Don't forget to include all loans: mortgages, auto loans, credit cards, student loans, personal debts, and consumer debt.

Don't feel too upset if you learn your net worth is negative. It is very common for a young physician to have a negative net worth because of their student loans. However, remember that your education is an asset, and student loans are an investment in your financial future.

If you fit into the negative net worth category, your first financial goal is to get your new worth back to zero. For you, it is especially important to establish a financial plan and get control of your financial life as soon as possible. But instead of dreading the process, have some fun with it. Celebrate and congratulate yourself when you become worthless, especially when you have worked hard to save, pay off debt and get on top of your finances.

Ignore the urge to put your head in the sand thinking you have no power over the situation. *You are not alone, and there's no reason to be embarrassed.* To prove it, you can take a look at our government. Their high federal deficit sets a dangerous precedent not only for our culture but also for the world's economy. No matter how big your debt problem, it looks relatively small in this light!

Simply make up your mind now to reverse the situation and be proud that you're taking the right steps. The obvious way to improve your net worth is to decrease your spending and/or increase your income and investments. Begin by taking a serious look at your spending habits and make sure you are doing everything you can to achieve first a zero, and eventually a positive, net worth. Getting yourself back to financial stability may feel like

Where Do I Start?

a long and lonely road, but with the help of a financial planner, you at least don't have to feel like you're doing it alone.

In summary, the most critical starting point to a financial plan is evaluating your net worth. Then, on a periodic basis, you can compare the results in order to establish trends and measure improvement. A convenient time to do this is once a year when you're doing your taxes. This way, all the paperwork is readily available and you're focused on your annual earnings and expenditures. Keep all the financial records together from each year's tax forms and net worth calculations for easy reference.

Your Budget

After calculating your net worth, you'll want to look at your monthly budget and define exactly where your money is being spent. The categories of the monthly budget should also include any deductions from your paycheck like state and federal income taxes, Social Security, and employee benefits. Once you have your take-home pay, you should deduct all of the fixed expenses and the estimated variable expenses.

Are you unable to account for where a large portion of your money goes? This is the case for many people. To overcome it, try a few or all of the following tips:

- Carry a pocket calendar with you for three months and record every cent you spend, no matter if it's for a candy bar, a cup of coffee, or the mortgage and car payment. Then tally it up and categorize it at the end of each month (some software programs, like *Quicken*, make this very easy) in order to see exactly where your paychecks are going.
- Vow to go back to the days of *cash only* transactions. For everything other than your large, monthly payments (and even those if you want to get really serious), stop using your debit and credit cards or writing checks for day-to-day expenditures like groceries, drugstore items, and clothing. It feels much different when you have to shell out $50 cash for a purchase than handing over a piece of plastic.

- Treat your savings account or investment amount as a bill you pay out every month like any other. Experience has shown that if you don't get in the habit of saving money on a regular basis, either through a payroll deduction or an automatic withdrawal from your checking account, the money you intended to go toward savings or investments is mysteriously spent elsewhere.

How quickly you can move toward financial security depends on how motivated you are to saving money. It's not easy for Americans to live on less than their income considering our credit-loving culture. However, if you start early enough, saving 15 percent of your gross income will typically be enough to help keep you safe from financial worries later on. If you are getting a later start, then you may need to be living on 75 to 80 percent of your income and saving 20 to 25 percent!

Saving or investing 15 percent of your income means you are able to live on 85 percent of your income. As elementary as this may sound, the significance is critical. In later years, this savings could accumulate to a substantial sum if invested properly. Also, it will teach you how to live below your means—a financial goal that seemingly every expert agrees upon, but few physicians live by.

Your Credit Score

Most physicians do not look at a high credit score as an asset. We think this is a mistake. An important long-term financial strategy should be to regularly monitor your credit score and make decisions that strengthen and improve it. While in practice, you should continue to utilize credit no matter how positive your cash flow. Some physicians are in a fortunate position that they never need to take out a loan again or utilize a credit card. This cash flow trap should be avoided, as it may come back to haunt you if/when if you apply for a mortgage on a second home, have a practice purchase/expansion, and/or co-sign a loan for someone.

The importance of credit and the significance of monitoring your credit score on a consistent basis cannot be understated. The financial information included in this report will be a huge factor on whether you can obtain a loan, get auto or home insurance, rent an apartment, or even apply for a job. Your

Where Do I Start?

credit score is often the most important factor in determining the rate at which you can obtain loans as well. The higher the score, the better off you will be. A higher score can be the difference in saving tens of thousands of dollars in interest throughout the duration of a loan.

As a starting point, we would suggest developing the habit of monitoring your credit score. It's a good idea to review your credit report at least once per year. We would suggest starting at www.annualcreditreport.com. Contact the credit bureaus, and correct any errors you find immediately. We recommend these frequent checks to monitor identity theft issues and accidentally missed payments that can have catastrophic effects on your credit score. The three credit bureaus are Equifax, Experian, and TransUnion, which all allow you to pull your credit report for free once a year. Each of these bureaus can contain a little different information and calculate your scores in slightly different ways.

A key aspect to the credit score is realizing what activity contributes to the score and to what degree they do. This is helpful to prioritize financial activity and decision-making as you take a proactive approach to improving and increasing your personal score.

- 35 percent of the score is developed from your *payment history*. You are penalized by payments occurring later than thirty days past due. The later you are, the more detrimental the effect on your score.
- 30 percent of your score is derived from your *credit utilization*. Ideally, the credit bureaus would like to see approximately 20 to 30 percent in use, with the first mark against you being made at 50 percent. This is the ratio of debt in use to debt available. This is on a per card/account basis.
- 15 percent of the final score comes from your *credit history*. This is concerned with how long you have the credit. Positive credit payment history stays on your score for 10 years, and a negative payment on credit as well as a positive payment on collection issues stays on for 7. (Keep open longstanding accounts even if you no longer use them. Closing these can hurt your score.)
- 10 percent of your score comes from the *types of credit used*—installment, revolving, etc. (looking for a solid mix).

- 10 percent of your score comes from *inquiries*. This involves recent searches for credit (not including free inquiries).

Source of percentages: FICO Credit Score Chart

Planning Tip: To maintain and keep (or raise) your credit score, it would be wise to finance a portion of a car, even if you have the cash to pay for it outright. Then, pay it off completely after thirteen monthly payments have been made. Or, take out a small loan (only if terms are favorable) or a credit card jointly with your college age child. This will help them establish their credit, utilization, and payment history. Plus, they may thank you when buying their first home or getting that first vehicle loan out of college as their credit scores are higher. Financially independent kids are a good investment!

3

The Pyramid

If you dumped all the pieces of a puzzle on a table, it is initially a daunting task to begin to put the puzzle together. Where do you start? Take one puzzle piece out of the pile at random, and it's hard to know where that piece fits into the big picture. It is much easier to put the puzzle together if you have a picture of what the scene will look like once completed. So, you look at the picture on the box to give you a guide to what the puzzle looks like when completed. We designed the financial pyramid as a method of seeing how a properly designed financial plan looks when it is put together correctly.

PYRAMID OF FINANCIAL NEEDS

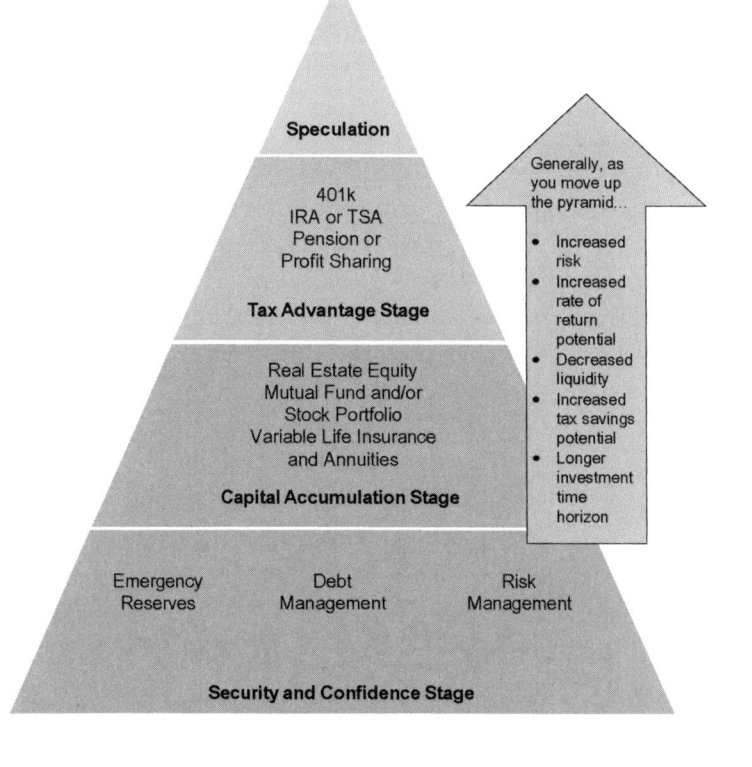

- Speculation
- 401k / IRA or TSA / Pension or Profit Sharing
  - **Tax Advantage Stage**
- Real Estate Equity / Mutual Fund and/or Stock Portfolio / Variable Life Insurance and Annuities
  - **Capital Accumulation Stage**
- Emergency Reserves | Debt Management | Risk Management
  - **Security and Confidence Stage**

Generally, as you move up the pyramid...
- Increased risk
- Increased rate of return potential
- Decreased liquidity
- Increased tax savings potential
- Longer investment time horizon

As you can see by the diagram, there are four main stages to the financial planning pyramid: *The Security and Confidence Stage*, *The Capital Accumulation Stage*, *The Tax-Advantaged Stage*, and *The Speculation Stage*.

The financial pyramid is a method of explaining the financial planning concept by categorizing your financial plan into stages. Of course, individual goals, habits, accomplishments, and so on are all unique, but most people share the same fundamental life stages. As a method of simply and efficiently organizing your financial life, the pyramid represents the key to financial independence and demonstrates the basic goal of increasing your assets and reducing your debt in order to have enough money invested to retire comfortably. Individuals may place more or less importance on one section of the pyramid than another, which is perfectly acceptable.

Without a doubt, organizing your finances in order to build a solid base is the first step. If you don't do this, you may be subjecting your financial situation to undue risk, which will cause problems later on. On the other hand, it's also important not to place too much emphasis on only one stage, neglecting the overall balance. This could be a sign of being overly conservative. As an example, not taking advantage of higher-potential returns in equity (stock) investments may mean losing your purchasing power in the long run, because the dollars may be worth less due to the effects of taxes and inflation.

It is very important to try and accomplish a lifelong financial balance. You certainly don't want to get to retirement age with a huge amount of money saved up, only to be in poor health and not be able to enjoy it. Especially, if that means you scrimped and saved your whole life working so hard that you didn't enjoy yourself along the way. By the same token, you don't want to be nearing retirement and realize you haven't saved enough and now must take a substantial drop in your standard of living or go back to work to simply survive. The ideal situation would be to retire at the same or a greater standard of living than that you were accustomed to in your working years, but not feel at any time that you have greatly sacrificed.

A fundamental of short- and long-term financial success is living on less than your income. If you can get used to living on 80 to 85 percent of your income, this allows you to commit 15 to 20 percent of your income to your net worth. Initially, this may mean aggressively paying off loans, but over time, the majority of this extra income should be saved. If you are living paycheck to paycheck, is there a way you can decrease your expenses and/or increase your income so you can start building some surplus funds into your monthly budget?

The ideal investment is completely liquid and has lots of tax advantages, a great rate of return, and low risk. If you find an advisor or salesman claiming to have such an investment, you would be wise to avoid them, as they are dangerous. This ideal investment does not exist. Let's use an analogy of spinning plates. If you have ever been to a circus or seen a juggler, you may have seen a performer attempt to spin a lot of plates on long sticks…all at the same time. The objective is to take limited energy and allocate it in such a manner as to keep all the plates spinning. It doesn't do any good to devote a lot of time to one spinning plate while the others are slowing down, wobbling, and falling down. The goal is to keep all the plates spinning!

Your financial plan is on somewhat the same level, with each financial decision representing a different plate. First of all, you need to find out which plates you want to start spinning and then direct your dollars to keep them going. You could have several debt reduction plates, some risk management (insurance) plates, retirement and/or college education plates, and so on. Each individual situation is going to be different. Again, there are limited resources that need to be allocated in such a way as to accomplish all of your goals. This is where the advice of a professional and experienced financial advisor can be very valuable.

The key financial variables in the pyramid are risk, liquidity, rate of return, and tax advantages. The money in your emergency reserves and at the *Security and Confidence Stage* should be very liquid or accessible. Generally, as you move to higher stages in the pyramid, the less liquid your funds become.

Risk and rate of return tend to go hand in hand. The higher the amount of risk you take, the higher the rate of return potential should be…given time. In the pyramid, typically lower risk with lower rates of return should be at the base of your planning and the risk and rate of return increase as you move up the pyramid. Historically, stock market and investing returns have less volatility the longer the time frame that is considered. Keep in mind, however, that past performance is not indicative of future results.

From a tax standpoint, there are typically not too many tax advantages at the lower level. If you have money in a savings account, that money is generating ordinary income on which you are paying tax, so there are no tax advantages there. On the other hand, when you put money into a qualified retirement plan, the contribution is on a before-tax basis, delaying and deferring the tax to a later date. Under most circumstances, however, you cannot touch the money in your qualified plan until age fifty-nine and a half without paying a 10 percent early withdrawal penalty plus the income taxes due on that amount. The rule of thumb on tax savings is similar to risk and rate of return. As you move up the pyramid, you'll have greater potential for tax advantages on your investments.

4

The Security and Confidence Stage

As you begin building a well-structured, sound financial plan, the first priorities are centered on three key issues. These issues represent the building blocks for your entire plan going forward. Regardless of what stage of financial planning you are in, it is critical that you:

- Maintain adequate emergency fund cash reserves
- Have debt under control and a structured system for repayment
- Have all insurance plans in effect

While the levels of each of these will vary significantly depending on the person, all sound financial plans have these three components in order. Each of these factors is equally important. Most people agree on the need to have money accessible for emergencies, to pay their debts, especially on high-interest credit cards, and to be adequately insured. The trick to the individual financial plan is to figure out the appropriate level for each of these.

1. Emergency Reserves

Does your financial agenda resemble that of Will Rogers as he said: *"I'm not so much concerned about the rate of return on my money, just the return of it."*

During your residency training, the primary *financial* objectives are to:

- Keep your debt under control as much as possible
- Try to live within (not beyond) your income
- Develop good financial planning habits
- Educate yourself

Perhaps the best "habit" to form that will continuously add value to a lifelong financial plan is keeping an adequate liquid cash emergency fund reserve. Regardless of where you are in your financial life, we advocate always maintaining an emergency fund reserve. Generally, a good rule of thumb is to add all of your total <u>fixed</u> monthly expenses and multiply by four or five. In the absence of any large, anticipated purchases or expenses within the next twelve to twenty-four months, this is an adequate amount to hold in cash as an emergency fund reserve. On a resident physician's salary, this is easier said than done! However, regardless of how tight your monthly budget is, we still advocate "paying yourself first" and each and every month contributing a fixed amount to a money market account. We recommend this even if the interest earned on a money market account is less than the interest being charged on a credit card or student loan debt.

Two very important things are accomplished with this. First, unexpected expenses that continuously happen at the worst time can be paid for without the entire bill being charged on a credit card. Second, you develop the habit of systematically saving a portion of income each and every month. This is a habit that will be of great value the rest of your life. It will be far easier to incrementally increase savings as your income increases, as opposed to being forced to increase your savings later in life.

Maintaining an adequate liquid cash reserve is just as important for the well-established, high-income medical specialist; the reasons are just a bit different.

Emergency Fund Reserves and Their Influence on Long-Term Rates of Return

A money market fund is essentially a mutual fund that invests in short term monetary instruments. It provides a relatively stable vehicle for your assets and generally offers higher return potential than a savings account. Also, money market funds often have check-writing privileges. They are a low risk investment that provides liquidity. The trade off for such liquidity and general stability of principal is, of course, a very low rate of return. While money market funds have a goal of stability, it's important to point out that they do have a slight degree of market risk. For the physician with a significant net worth, a high income, and a high level of financial security, the low return on a money market fund isn't very appealing and often leads

The Security and Confidence Stage

to inadequate emergency fund reserves. When the unexpected expense arises, other assets with greater degrees of price fluctuation must be tapped. Should these other, more volatile assets be liquidated at an inopportune time, the consequences can be devastating.

Consider the following:

$10,000 invested over a fifteen year period ending December 31, 2009, in a hypothetical investment that performed similarly to the unmanaged S&P 500, would have experienced the following results:

- Fully invested for entire period $31,917
- Missed the best ten days $15,928
- Missed the best twenty days $ 9,990
- Missed the best thirty days $ 6,690
- Missed the best forty days $ 4,595
- Missed the best sixty days $ 2,355

results based on S&P 500 composite index without reinvested dividends. The S&P 500 is an unmanaged group of stocks representative of the market in general. You cannot invest directly into an index. An index does not have fees which would reduce returns. Past performance does not guarantee future returns. Investments will fluctuate and when redeemed, may be worth more or less than when originally purchased.

Withdrawing investments originally intended for longer time horizons at a bad time can have a huge impact on your rate of return. Just a few days "out of the market" can essentially ruin a perfectly prudent, well-structured, and properly allocated investment portfolio's rate of return. Adequate liquid cash reserves will allow longer-term investments to remain just that, long-term investments!

The one constant in life is that there will always be surprises. The purpose of an emergency reserve fund is just what it sounds like—money that is very accessible when you really need it. The main characteristic of an investment in this category would be the money that is liquid yet invested in more stable vehicles so the principal remains intact. The most common mistake people make here is not having adequate reserves or taking undue risk with these funds. This money needs to remain liquid in case of unexpected expenses like car expenses, home repairs, job loss, or medical emergencies.

For most people, the main benefit of having an adequate emergency reserve fund is access to funds when needed. When you are financially prepared for these surprises, they become less stressful and are therefore easier to deal with emotionally. Furthermore, when there is a source of funds for these types of emergencies, you do not have to rely on credit cards or personal, unsecured, high-interest loans.

A money market mutual fund is often the best choice as an emergency reserve possibility. Many people incorrectly associate the term mutual fund with high risk. However, a mutual fund only has as much risk as the underlying investments it owns. A money market mutual fund pools investors' dollars in the typical mutual fund style and purchases jumbo CDs through banks, treasury securities (T bills), as well as commercial paper. Most money market funds have a check writing privilege, which allows you to write checks against your account subject to minimums of usually $250 or $500. The rate of return earned on these funds will fluctuate based on the short-term money market but is typically competitive with the interest rate at the time. **Investments in a money market fund are neither insured nor guaranteed by the FDIC or any government agency. Although the fund seeks to preserve the value of your investment at $1 per share, it is possible to lose money by investing in the fund.**

Life insurance cash values on permanent policies (i.e., whole life, adjustable life, universal life) can also be important sources of emergency reserve funds. These funds are typically earning a competitive fixed rate of return, and they are accessible. It is usually possible to take out a loan or borrow against your cash value, using it as collateral; or sometimes you can take an outright withdrawal of this money. Remember, though, that any loans or withdrawals taken will reduce both your policy cash value and death benefit. Also, please remember that the primary reason to purchase a life insurance policy is the death benefit. A thorough discussion of this is found in chapter 6.

A home equity line of credit is another option. With equity in your house, interest rates low and tax deductible, this option should not be discounted. In fact, in periods of time when there is a low interest rate environment, maintaining an open line of credit against your house equity can be a viable source of emergency reserve cash. It could also be used to pay down a high-interest credit card or for a major purchase like a car. The drawback is that

The Security and Confidence Stage 31

it needs to be paid off when you sell your house, which of course would result in fewer proceeds at closing. If your house would decline in value, creating less equity, you may have to pay off the home equity line and/or face a higher interest rate on the loan. While interest rates on home equity loans are higher than a few years ago, this may still be an option worth considering, especially if you can use the money to pay off higher-interest consumer debt. Please note, the terms of home equity line of credit arrangements are controlled by the lending institution and should be reviewed with your legal advisor.

2. Debt Management

If you are in the fortunate situation of having no debts, congratulations! If you come from the school of thought that you don't ever want to owe anything to anybody, debt management is not an issue. However, in today's society this ideology is very uncommon and many people could use some strategies on effectively managing their debt.

Financially, it would make sense to rank all of your debts from highest to lowest interest, paying attention to the after-tax cost of borrowing. Since consumer debt is not tax deductible, those rates are taken at face value. However, a mortgage or home equity loan is deductible, so the real rate of return is the after-tax cost.

To give another general rule of thumb, credit cards and consumer debt would be the first to pay off if they have the highest interest rates. Then you would want to work away at the furniture loan, the used car loan, the new car loan, student loans, and finally the home mortgage. Nowadays, there are many credit cards that offer very low interest rates on balance transfers, which can be a temporary solution. But beware that the rate after the introductory period is not actually higher than your current card.

It is also important to look at debt management from a cash flow standpoint as well as an emotional standpoint. With this in mind, it can make sense to pay off a lower-interest loan if it will improve your cash flow dramatically, or if emotionally it is important for you to get it paid off for some other reason. Many people find a sense of satisfaction in paying debts off completely. Once one debt is paid off, take the extra cash and immediately begin paying off another loan more aggressively so that cash does not get absorbed into the budget.

If in your training years, you should also look in to income based repayment (IBR) which allows you to make payments that are relative to your income. The rules on IBR change periodically. Currently, the payment to loans is capped at 15% of your discretionary income. For the most up to date details, visit www.student.ed.gov. and type IBR in the search box.

3. Risk Management

Protecting yourself against unforeseen catastrophic losses is the third critical area of the base of the pyramid and the *Security and Confidence Stage*. In fact, think of this as a three-legged stool. Kick one leg out, and the stool will not stand. The financial pyramid is just like that.

Important insurance coverage can include health and major medical, auto, disability, long-term care, and homeowners or renters. In many cases, life and/or disability insurance are overlooked. However, these can be very important depending on your personal situation.

The reason for placing risk management at this point is obvious. You need to protect yourself from losses that would create such a hole that you may otherwise never dig yourself out. Then, once you are on your way to financial independence, insurance plays an equally important role in protecting your assets.

While you don't want to have any gaps in your insurance protection, you certainly don't want to overlap or duplicate coverage. The ideal financial plan will have you paying reasonable premium levels while providing maximum protection. Remember, the major role of insurance is to protect against catastrophic losses. A common mistake is trying to insure too many contingencies or not using deductibles to your advantage.

You will want to ask yourself a couple of questions before purchasing insurance:

- Is the premium for this coverage going to dramatically affect my lifestyle?

- If I do not buy this coverage and suffer the losses that would have been covered, would I be in grave financial trouble?

If the answer to the first question is *no* and to the second *yes,* then the insurance in question is right for you. If not, reconsider the structure and price of the insurance. Consult an experienced financial professional to help you determine the appropriate levels of coverage and how to structure your insurance within the context of a comprehensive financial plan. We also believe life and disability insurance are so important for the physician that we are devoting the next two chapters to these topics.

Looking back to the Middle Ages, we get a glimpse of the importance of insurance. People of wealth built fabulous castles and filled them with treasures. They always devoted significant resources to protecting those assets in the form of an army, a moat, and so on. In a sense, that was an early form of an insurance policy. So, as you continue to build your net worth, you should review and update your insurance to be sure you are maximizing your coverage and protecting you and your family and your wealth

For starters, we recommend making sure you have the basics covered. Health insurance, auto insurance and renters/home owners insurance. This will serve as the base level to your risk management corner of the pyramid before you acquire other types of coverage.

Umbrella Liability Coverage

If you are ever sued, your standard homeowners or auto policy will provide you with *some* liability coverage. It will pay for judgements against you and your attorney's fees, up to a limit set in the policy. But you may want to have an extra layer of liability protection, which is what an umbrella policy does.

An umbrella policy kicks in when you reach the limit on the underlying liability coverage in a homeowners', renters', condo or auto policy. It will also cover you for things such as libel and slander.

Because the personal umbrella policy goes into effect after the underlying coverage is exhausted; there are certain limits that usually must be met in order to purchase this coverage. Most insurers will want you to have a minimum of $250,000 of liability insurance on your auto policy and $300,000 of liability insurance on your homeowners policy before selling you umbrella liability $1 million of additional coverage.

This amount does vary by carrier; however, for about $150 per year, you can buy a $1 million policy. The policy can be increased in million dollar increments. Generally speaking, umbrella liability coverage is cheapest when you purchase it with your homeowners', renters' and auto insurance.

5

Disability Income Insurance

Unless you are independently wealthy, your ability to earn an income is your greatest financial asset. Protecting this income should be a primary objective of every financial plan. Therefore, a thorough understanding of disability insurance and all of its features is a fundamental objective of this book.

What Is Disability Insurance?

Disability insurance is insurance on your greatest financial asset, your income. This is an especially important insurance policy for the high-income specialist. Given the numbers of years spent on education and training, your skills are very unique. If a sickness or accident occurs that renders you unable to perform these unique skills, disability insurance is what allows you to stay in your home, pay your bills, and continue to provide for your family's financial needs.

A disability income policy must have features and benefits that match your unique skills and fulfill the intended purpose of replacing income in the event of disability. Here is an explanation of the features and benefits that should be considered.

How Is the Disability Defined?

The definition of a disability is perhaps the most important feature of a policy. We suggest using a policy that has true "own occupation" specialty specific coverage. If you are unable to practice your unique skills, the resulting loss of income is replaced. However, there are several different levels of "own occupation" coverage.

- *True own occupation*: A policy that has "true own occupation" will pay the stated benefit of the disability policy if you cannot perform the exact duties of your occupation. The policy would continue to pay the full benefits of the contract even if you were able to work and generate an income. If you are not working in your exact field, the policy pays. A neurosurgeon unable to practice neurosurgery due to an accident or sickness but is able to work in an administrative position would receive the full disability benefit. Furthermore, if that same neurosurgeon started a business and eventually earns more than he or she was earning as a neurosurgeon, he or she would still receive the full benefits with a true own occupation disability plan.

A policy with true own occupation coverage will typically be more expensive. Such an "ironclad" definition of a disability is a very important feature to consider, especially with physicians who have sub-specialty training. The greater the amount of training and the more specialized you become, the greater the need for a true own occupation policy.

- *Transitional occupation*: A policy that has a "transitional own occupation" definition is a bit different than the above "true own occupation." If you cannot practice your duties due to an accident or sickness, a policy with this type of definition would pay the stated benefit for as long as you are disabled. Your unique duties and skills are covered. The difference in the two policy definitions becomes evident if you retrain and return to work in another field. With a regular occupation definition, the disability benefits would begin to be reduced as income from another occupation increases. Should this income from another occupation exceed the income you generated as a medical specialist, the disability benefits would cease. Such a definition of disability will have a lower premium than the above "true own occupation."

Future Insurability Options – It is easy to see why disability insurance is so important within a sound financial plan. However, a resident physician earning $50,000 per year with no other sources of income, a mortgage payment, car payment, and a spouse at home with children may not have enough disposable income to purchase a large disability policy. Thus, one of

Disability Income Insurance

the more important disability policy features that any physician should consider is a future purchase or future insurability option. This feature allows for the insured to increase the amount of disability coverage in the future, when income is higher, without having to prove medical insurability.

Let's look at an example of why this type of feature can have a real-life impact.

One of our young radiology residents had a wife who worked at home managing the household, and his salary at the time was about $50,000 per year. His situation was a bit unique for two reasons. First, he was very fortunate not to have any student loans. Second, he was able to supplement his income with regular moonlighting. Even with the two exceptions, their monthly cash flow was tight and they were unwilling to consider disability insurance, viewing it as yet another expense they could do without. It was, in their minds, a simple question of priorities. Besides, he was young and healthy, and in just a few short years his income in private practice would be much higher and he would worry about disability insurance at that time.

We were unable to convince them of the importance of protecting their future income.

Fast forward three years to the end of his residency training. Upon completion of residency, he was offered his dream job in his (and his wife's) hometown of Detroit. They were both very excited to finally be done living check to check, be closer to family, and move on with the next phase of life. They had big plans as well, all of which were dependent upon his income. There was one small hitch with the radiology group he joined; they did not offer any group long-term disability. This meant he would be forced to cover his income entirely through individual disability insurance.

The thought of having no income protection, with so many plans they had made, was a risk they could not afford to take. An accident, sickness, or some ailment that would prevent him from practicing radiology could mean many of their dreams going up in smoke.

During the underwriting process, he learned he had adult onset diabetes. This was the first he knew of his condition, and it meant from a disability insurance standpoint that he would be uninsurable forever. He and his wife determined that being unable to protect his income was too great a risk. They took a different job with a different group that had a group long-term disability plan.

As a member of the group, he automatically received coverage under the group long-term disability plan. Even though the coverage amount was less than half of his income, it was something. Although the job was still in Detroit, it was much further away, with lower pay, and in a less-than-ideal environment for him.

The inability to protect his income could have been avoided, had he purchased an individual disability policy with a future income protection rider that allowed him to increase his coverage when he entered private practice without evidence of medical insurability.

A medical specialist looking to protect his or her income but unwilling or unable to afford a large disability premium at the present time could purchase a disability policy that protects their current income with a future purchase option or future insurability agreement (different companies have different names) that gives them the guaranteed ability to increase coverage in the future. Many companies will allow up to an additional $5,000 a month of benefit, no medical questions asked. The cost of this feature adds an additional $12 to $17 a month or so to the monthly premium. This is a very low cost to guarantee your ability to increase coverage in the future.

Residual/Partial Disability Benefits – Many disabilities are not total and complete. The residual disability benefit feature would pay a monthly benefit should you suffer a partial loss of income. There are very few, if any, group long-term disability plans that have such a feature. Under most group plans, you must be completely and totally disabled and under the constant care of a physician in order to receive a disability benefit.

For example, a radiologist who loses the use of her hand and is unable to perform interventional procedures but can still read film and perform many of the normal duties would qualify. If her interventional procedures were responsible for a significant portion of income, the loss of such income can still have a devastating effect on her financial life. Any individual disability policy should have a rider that would pay a percentage of income lost resulting from a partial disability.

Non-Cancelable/Guaranteed Renewable – We recommend disability policies that are non-cancelable and guaranteed renewable. This means as long as you pay your premium on time, the company cannot cancel your coverage or raise your rates. Given the importance of disability coverage and knowing it will be a policy you own for many years, no change in your premium cost or coverage can provide real peace of mind and should always be a feature of your disability plan.

Cost of Living Adjustment – This particular feature becomes extremely beneficial for disabilities that are more long term. This feature protects the benefits net purchasing power against inflation once one qualifies for claim. A common COLA on a physician's disability policy is 3%.

Exclusions – Ideally, insurance policies would not have loopholes, exclusions, or preexisting exclusion riders. Coverage would be guaranteed under any and all circumstances. This is not the case. When analyzing your disability insurance needs, you must consider your area of specialty, understand the exclusions that may exist on the policy, and determine if they are acceptable.

If the policy has exclusions, will your income still be, under most circumstances, adequately covered? This is a difficult question and will vary greatly from one medical specialty to another. Our advice to our physician clients is to look at the exclusion and determine if it is reasonable given their specialty.

If the policy has all the features and benefits necessary to adequately cover your income in your particular specialty and the exclusion is highly unlikely to be an issue, the coverage is acceptable. If not, look at another company that may have a slightly inferior policy but does not have the same exclusion. Perhaps an example best sums it up:

Many (not all) companies have a mental and nervous exclusion. Policies with such an exclusion would treat a disability related to depression or anxiety differently than a muscular or skeletal accident. If your disability is due to depression, many disability companies would only pay a benefit for a limited period of time, typically twenty-four months, after which, if you are still not working due to depression-related issues, the disability benefit would stop.

It is very important to understand the exclusions, know when they may come into play, and determine if they are acceptable given the other features and benefits of contract.

Conclusion

Without a doubt, a correctly structured disability policy is a critical element in any physician's financial plan. Over the years, we have witnessed many examples of this. Uninsured, disabled physicians have let us know that they wish their advisors had been more adamant about purchasing a policy as we described.

Insured, disabled physicians have been able to continue being paid, children can remain in the same schools, life can go on, and all energy and focus can be directed where it should be; and that is dealing with the disability and recovery, not worrying about finances.

6

Life Insurance

The subject of life insurance is very confusing to physicians because there are so many products and solutions AND opinions. Just a quick google search and you will see thousands of articles, websites, and links. Unfortunately, this can lead to information that is biased or skewed in one way or another. In this chapter, we will attempt to educate and simplify this decision and provide you with a decision tree that you can use.

As mentioned earlier in the book, a successful financial plan provides financial strength and confidence, and minimizes worry and stress. In addition…options and choices to enhance and compliment a comprehensive financial plan. Life insurance, as a properly structured component of a comprehensive plan, not only provides dollars to spouses, partners, children and heirs, but depending on the type of policy, can also provide some of the following:

-Protect your insurability in the event of a health change

-Security for a job change rather than rely on group benefits for all your coverage

-A source of cash for emergencies and/or opportunities[1]

-Guarantee the ability to convert to a permanent product as your cash flow allows[2]

-Allow for continuation of coverage during a long term disability if a waiver of premium for disability clause is added to the policy[2]

-Use the cash value early in the event of a long term care need[3]

-Cash values grows tax deferred and if structured correctly (we'll address that later in the chapter), can be used in a tax favored manner

-Asset protection…in some states, the cash value is an exempt asset from claims of creditors[4]

-Estate planning uses help you to maximize the estate left to your heirs and charities

-secure a bank loan and/or buy out a deceased partner in a business

[1] *Policy loans and withdrawals may create an adverse tax result in the event of a lapse or policy surrender, and will reduce both the cash value and death benefit.*
[2] *Terms and Conditions vary by product and provider*
[3] *This feature is generally available through an optional rider, and is available for an additional fee and restrictions and limitations may apply.*
[4] *Applicability may be subject to restrictions. Consult a local attorney.*

How Much Life Insurance Do You Need?

Please see the graph below for a visual discussion of a typical person's need for life insurance. The solid line labeled "A" illustrates that at an early age, you may not need any (or not much) coverage. As you get older, you may be in a relationship, start a family, take on a mortgage, and/or buy into a practice, and your need for life insurance increases. How much coverage you need and how long this lasts is due to a lot of variables and everyone is different. But, there is an economic and emotional toll that your death may present and life insurance is the most economical method of addressing this.

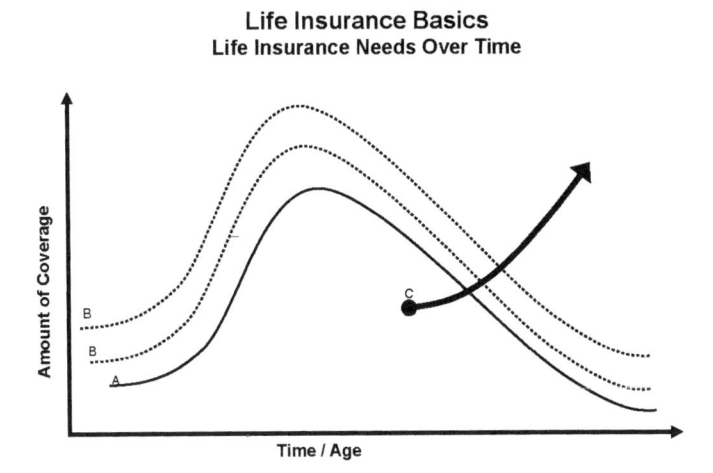

Life Insurance

Life Insurance Basics
Life Insurance Needs Over Time

[Graph showing Amount of Coverage vs. Time/Age, with curves labeled A and B (dotted lines), and point C marked with an upward arrow]

As you get older, typically your needs start to decrease...as you pay off debts, you build other assets, and your children become self sufficient (hopefully!). And, in fact, many people would look at this graph and conclude that they may not need any life insurance at they get older. Conceptually, this makes sense. Especially for people who are debt free, and have built up a substantial asset base. However, the dotted lines (labeled B) illustrate the fact that this insurance need line goes up every year due to inflation.

The point labeled "C" triggers an interesting situation. People who are very successful financially and frankly financially independent (and may not need life insurance for the original reasons) my want to keep (or buy new) coverage as a very effective method of paying estate taxes so that the estate that they have built more efficiently transfers to heirs or charities. Or, owning a life insurance policy at retirement can act as a "permission slip" to be more aggressive in living on the principle of your investments knowing that the death benefit provided due to a premature death replaces those assets to your survivors depending on those assets.

As for how much you may need, this is an interesting topic. Think about the following statements and see if any of them applies to your thinking?

"My partner (or spouse) has a good job and should be able to continue to work if I die, so I probably don't need much coverage."

"I have all the coverage I need through work/my employer/my group."

"I'm a stay at home (mom or dad) and do not bring in any income, so I do not need any life insurance."

"I'm single right now and not in a relationship and therefore don't have any dependents, so why would I consider life insurance at this point in my life?"

"Why would I ever consider insuring my children?"

"I have read that cash value life insurance is a bad investment and that you should never combine the two."

Frankly, we have heard all of these comments and many more. Hopefully, the following discussion will help you understand this complicated product, and decision. Once understood, we think you will see the needs met, and valuable benefits provided by life insurance and not view it as a "necessary evil" like other insurance purchases.

The maximum you can buy is based on your "Human Life Value". Each insurance company uses a different calculation, but essentially the total is about twenty to thirty times your annual income. Essentially, this is the present value of your lifetime income stream. Ideally, if life insurance was free, we would all obtain this amount, wouldn't you agree?

Since it is not free and most people are juggling many competing goals with their finances, a decision has to be made. How much coverage should I (you) buy? Essentially, tally up all the debts you have, any lump sums of cash you want to provide (emergency fund for survivors, college funds for kids, etc.) and then add that total to the present value of the stream of income that would be needed to go to your heirs at your death. (factor in their working ability, your confidence in social security, etc.). A competent financial advisor can work through this calculation with you. Usually, the resulting number suggests obtaining between seven and fifteen times your annual income depending on all the variables.

Types of Life Insurance Coverage

Essentially, there are two types of life insurance...term and permanent. Term coverage is much like all other insurance coverage you may purchase. If you die, they pay a death claim. If the coverage lapses or is discontinued, there is no further value. Permanent life insurance on the other hand, may build cash value. There are many types of permanent policies and this is where the confusion often starts.

Look at the graph (T). This is essentially a mortality curve and term life insurance is priced based on such a mortality curve. You can buy a ten, twenty or even thirty year term policy where the rate is level for that time, but if you wanted to renew beyond that point, the rates would go up exponentially. Term insurance is very appropriate for someone who has a short term need for life insurance (generally ten years or less) or has a very high need for coverage but can't afford a permanent policy. Also, a convertible (the ability to convert from term to permanent without evidence of good health) term policy is very appropriate for young physicians as a way to secure some coverage for a small premium, while you are healthy and the rates are low.

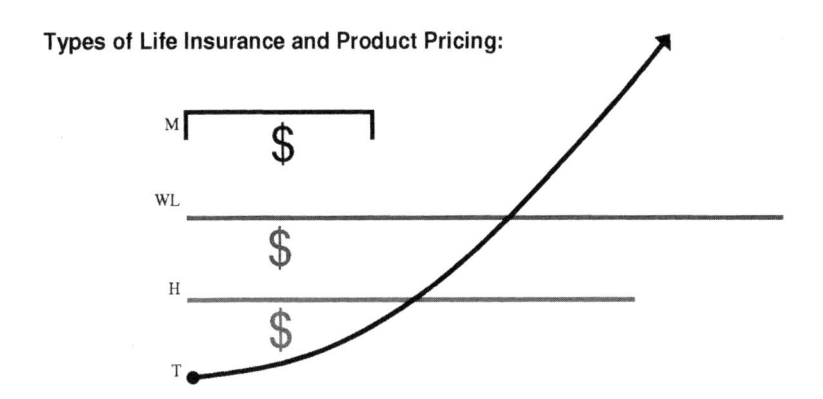

Types of Life Insurance and Product Pricing:

*This is a very generic and simplified graph to illustrate the annual premium pricing differences between the main types of products. Individual circumstances and product design, coordinated by a knowledgeable and experienced advisor will determine the final numbers.

As for permanent life insurance, there are many marketing names and varieties of policies, but for practical purposes in this book, we will outline the two most common; whole life and a "hybrid" policy. While products vary by provider, a simplified way to look at the whole life (Whole life WL) is that was developed many years ago as an alternative to term insurance. The premium is much more expensive than term in the early years, but level throughout your whole life. Because you are paying more for the coverage than the pure risk while you are young, "cash value" is created for the purpose of helping to offset the increasing cost of coverage later in life. This is then what helps support the cost for the life insurance when you are older and the cost for insurance is actually more than the premium you are paying. If you pay enough into the whole life policy, it can become paid up.

Some advantages of whole besides offering lifetime coverage are that the cash values grow on a tax deferred basis, can be surrendered if needed, could be used as collateral if you need to borrow against them. This multi-purpose asset has gained in popularity in recent years because the cash values grow from one year to the next based on a crediting rate paid by the insurance company.

The disadvantages of whole life are also numerous. These policies are not very flexible. If you need to make changes to the policy, (raising or lowering the death benefit or the premium amount) this can be cumbersome or impossible depending on the company. Many companies would rather sell you a new policy rather than make changes to an existing policy potentially resulting in new or higher fees and commissions. We have run into people who have a dozen policies duplicating policy fees, which is inefficient knowing that other "hybrid" products exist. For people who are very conservative, have quite a bit of discretionary cash flow, are not comfortable investing into anything that has market risk, and have a need to ensure a death benefit for their entire life, a whole life policy may be appropriate.

The "hybrid" (H) policy is another option in which the annual premium generally falls somewhere between term and whole life. This can vary quite a bit, and in general, the higher the premium, the more the opportunity for more cash value…resulting in the policy remaining in force for a longer period of time. The graph above illustrates a premium payment and coverage lasting until retirement age. There are many different hybrid policies which confuses the subject even more. Usually, the premium is

Life Insurance

flexible and changeable, the death benefit can vary as your needs change, and there are a variety of methods of crediting the cash value accounts. In general, this flexible choice can be used to implement a part of a financial plan that is monitored frequently by the policy owner and a trusted financial advisor.

Very conservative investors used to gravitate towards fixed life policies. An indexed product allows for potential upside (with limitations) connected to a common benchmark (such as the S&P 500 index) while the downside is protected. A variable life policy allows the policy owner to build a portfolio often choosing between numerous sub accounts. You can be as conservative or aggressive as your own needs and circumstances allow. Of course, this carries market risk that is not present in traditional fixed or indexed insurance products. Because of all of the options, working with an experienced advisor who knows you and your circumstances and risk tolerance, is recommended.

When a policy is funded at a much higher level, it can build more cash value and in some cases become paid up. (See graph labeled M.) There is an IRS calculation based on your age, and death benefit amount which determines the maximum premium you can pay without the policy becoming a Modified Endowment Contract (MEC), which then loses some valuable benefits. Figuring out how much you want to contribute to a policy for all your personal reasons (tax deferred growth, asset protection, funding for kids college, and/or retirement supplement, etc.), and then solving for the least amount of death benefit you need to have will result in a situation where the policy looks best for the long term "living" reasons. Again, we cannot emphasize this enough, please work with a very competent agent or advisor on these matters as a mistake here, could "taint" your policy and you could lose some of the very valuable tax benefits.

For most physicians, a combination of a hybrid policy and term insurance is the most economical and efficient way to cover your lifetime life insurance needs and use your life insurance for many other financial purposes.

Variable life insurance is sold only by prospectus. The prospectus contains important information about the product's investment objectives, charges and expenses, as well as the risks and other

information associated with the product. You may obtain a copy of the prospectus from your representative. You should carefully consider the risks and investment charges of a specific product before investing. You should always read the prospectus carefully before investing.

Variable life insurance products contain fees, such as management fees, fund expenses, distribution fees and mortality and expense charges. The variable investment options are subject to market risk, including loss of principal.

Policy loans and withdrawals may create an adverse tax result in the event of a lapse or policy surrender, and will reduce both the cash value and death benefit.

If a policy is over funded and becomes a modified endowment contract (MEC), the contract's earnings will be taxed as ordinary income at withdrawal, and may be subject to a 10% penalty if withdrawn before age 59 1/2.

Please keep in mind that the primary reason to purchase a life insurance product is the death benefit.

7

The Capital Accumulation Stage

This stage represents a large amount of assets you will build up over your lifetime. The assets that tend to comprise this stage are quite varied. Some of the investments include individual stocks and bonds, mutual funds, variable life insurance cash values, and equity in real estate or a business. Aside from the equity you build into your retirement plan, the majority of your financial independence will come from these investments. While these assets can also serve as emergency reserves, the investment horizon is usually five years or longer.

For many Americans, one of the most substantial forms of saving is simply making a monthly payment on your home. Generally speaking, real estate has long been a favorite investment tool for its tax benefits and as a buffer against inflation. Although there can be significant investment benefits in the long term, buying real estate is not without its risks. Deflation and poor housing markets may decrease property values, or suspected long-term growth in a given area may not occur. Changes in tax law may reduce or eliminate anticipated tax benefits. Also, real estate is not liquid, so the necessity of a quick sale may require a substantial reduction in price.

As for setting up an investment portfolio…diversify, diversify, diversify! Nothing else will be as crucial to your portfolio as diversifying and having a long-term plan. It's important to diversity not only by asset class but also by tax treatment and time horizon. We all know the proverb, "Don't put all your eggs in one basket." Well, take it to the extreme—don't put all the baskets on the same truck, and don't drive all the trucks down the same road! It's not necessary to look too far back to recall the faddish investing in technology and startup internet companies of the late 1990s. Too many investors lost too much when the overvalued stocks plunged and those eager investors expecting big returns were left with substantial losses. Most financial planners utilize a comprehensive questionnaire that helps you to identify your risk tolerance, and ultimately your asset allocation policy. Be sure to ask your advisor for such a tool.

Let's explore the most important discussion points as you begin to develop your investment philosophy.

Investment Planning: Information Versus Wisdom

Over the years, we have seen many market cycles, wars, natural disasters, terrorist attacks, low interest rates, high interest rates, and innumerable other factors that have influenced our physician clients' investment performance. But what factors have had the biggest influence on long-term investment planning? What factors have led to success? What factors have contributed to failure? What are the prudent time-tested investment strategies that will likely have the most positive influence on your overall long-term performance?

While there are many factors that influence your investment success or failure, here is a brief summary of issues we believe have the most potential to influence your long-term success.

Diversify

There are many factors that influence the performance of a particular investment from one year to the next. Individual asset class performance can vary so much from year to year that trying to predict results will likely lead to poor decisions. A portfolio well diversified among many asset categories will have lower volatility and provide better potential for a more steady performance. Your overall returns may not be the highest or lowest in any given period, but by keeping volatility levels in check in the short term, you will reduce the likelihood of making irrational decisions that can have very harmful effects on your long-term returns.

Sometimes misunderstood, the main goal of diversification is not to maximize your return but to minimize your risk and lower your volatility. The basic premise is that there is as much risk in being out of the market

The Capital Accumulation Stage

when it goes up as being in the market when it goes down, especially for your long-term money. While diversification does not guarantee against loss, it is a method used to manage risk.

Time...Not Timing

You can take something very volatile, like the annual returns in the stock market, and help manage that volatility by adding the element of time. While past performance is not a guarantee of future results, historically, the longer the timeframe considered, generally, the less volatile an investment becomes. So, one of the most important considerations for your financial plan is to keep your short-tem (less than eighteen months) money away from the stock market and allocate your long-term (greater than ten years) money to a well-diversified portfolio of mostly equities.

Avoid Mainstream Media Sensationalism

If you were to make investment decisions based on the nightly news, CNBC, or the daily newspaper, not only would you be destined for investment failure, but maybe even total destitution! This is <u>not</u> due to the inaccuracy of information being provided by such sources, but rather the dramatization of <u>short-term</u> events that have little or no impact on long-term investment strategies!

Taking information that is reported daily and using it for decisions with long-term money can have devastating consequences. This is compounded significantly by the ease with which you can simply log on to your brokerage account, 401k, or any other investment account and make changes on a daily basis.

Money invested for the long term should not be managed like it is needed next week. It must be managed with a long-term perspective.

Managing Behavior and Decisions

When discussing average rates of return over longer periods, it is important to differentiate between the average rate of return for the *investor* and that of the *fund*. The rate of return for the specific fund does not necessarily translate to the individual investor earning the same rate of return. An illustration can best emphasize this point on the futility of chasing rates of return.

As reported by the Wall Street Journal on December 31, 2009, the CGM Focus Fund was the best performing equity fund throughout the decade that had just ended. This was the "lost decade" as it has been described by some because the S&P 500 index had a compounded loss over the same timeframe. The CGM Focus Fund had an average rate of return of 18% per year. Yet, the average investor experienced an 11% LOSS! Why? They invested in the fund after a run up in value, chasing past returns, and sold when the fund was down, guaranteeing and locking in their losses. This is exactly the behavior that one should avoid.

This example is being used for illustrative purposes only, and is not a recommendation to invest in the CGM Focus Fund. Generally, potential for higher return is accompanied by a higher risk of loss. A fund's risks, expenses, investment objectives and other information is available in the fund's prospectus. You should carefully consider the risks and investment charges of a specific product and carefully read the prospectus before investing.

Source: *Wall Street Journal, 12-31-2009*

Don't Concentrate on a Specific Asset Category

It is easy to pick on the scores of investors who were caught up in the tech boom of the late 1990s. Those who invested so heavily in technology and became significantly over-weighted in one asset category then suffered devastating losses during the market down turn of 2000 to 2003.

It is so easy, in fact, that we won't. But what about investment periods of one, three, and five years during which the performance variation between different asset categories are more subtle? What is the best method to manage a portfolio over time without getting too concentrated in one asset category or not having enough in another?

The first step is to diversify! There are many methods that exist to help determine an appropriate allocation given your specific time horizon, risk

The Capital Accumulation Stage

tolerance levels, and overall investment objectives. This process requires much thought and discussion, but ultimately an allocation will emerge. What percentage of your investments should be allocated towards various asset categories, large cap growth, large cap value, international, fixed income, small cap, and so on.

Throughout the years, it is critical to monitor this allocation and determine where it is appropriate to perhaps alter new contributions or possibly even trim down one asset category to buy another. The main objective with regularly monitoring a diversified portfolio is twofold:

- Keep target allocations in line with original allocations, making it less likely to become over- or under-weighted in one asset category. This will decrease the likelihood of investment decisions made based on emotions.
- Do not over-monitor! The ease with which one can make changes to any investment makes not reacting to short-term fluctuations all the more difficult. By regularly monitoring and discussing the portfolio, you can know where one particular fund is in the overall picture and determine a reasonable time or specific share price to reallocate.

Don't Expect Everything From One Investment

This is a long-winded equivalent to diversification. Building a prudent, well-structured investment portfolio consists of having exposure to assets with potential for big gains over time, while at the same time exposure to assets that perform consistently during good times while helping to limit losses in bad times.

Having a mix of stock and bonds is critical to lower levels of volatility over time. A well-allocated mix of investments would consist of exposure to the following broad asset categories:

- Growth stocks: large, medium, and small (1: see page 60)
- Value stocks: large, medium, and small
- International stocks (2): developed countries, emerging markets

- Fixed income: corporate bonds, government bonds, high yield bonds (4)
- Real estate securities (3): low correlation with stocks

What percentage exposure you have to each type of asset category will depend on your time horizon, risk profile, and overall objectives. Once your allocation is established, regular monitoring and periodic rebalancing will be critical in helping to accomplish the two most important objectives: lower levels of short-term volatility while pursuing the highest potential for long-term rate of return.

Get Help from a Professional

While we like to think and tell our clients how good we are at "picking" the right investments, this is not how an investment professional adds real, meaningful value. Yes, a true professional is generally better equipped to analyze investment vehicles more thoroughly than the average physician, but this is not what will have the biggest influence on your investment rate of return. An investment where an advisor can provide great value is through a fee-based Investment Advisory account.

So, where and how does an advisor add real value?

An area in which your financial advisor will add significant value to your investment planning is helping deal with emotional decisions. A financial advisor worth their weight in gold is one who is not afraid to tell you "No" when it comes to making investment decisions based on emotion. It is your hard-earned money and your future, and you are emotionally attached to it. When the value investment goes up in one quarter or even a year, you cannot help but want to buy more of it. What better "source" for this than selling an investment *down* in value during this same time period. This strategy for decision-making based predominately on a short-term trend and/or a "gut feeling" will almost certainly lead to disappointing long-term returns.

Your advisor should take the time to discuss the specifics as to why each fund is performing the way it is during this short time period, what it means

The Capital Accumulation Stage

to the overall objective of your portfolio, and whether any decisions to buy or sell some or all of the fund need to be made.

Many times in our experience, just talking a bit further about a particular fund's performance and gaining a better understanding of why the performance has been what it is will be enough to avoid emotional and many times irrational decisions that may have a devastating effect on your long-term performance.

Your advisor should regularly update you on your portfolio progress, review your *current* asset allocation with that of your *target* allocation, and discuss potential adjustments that should be made. Adjustments to your investment portfolio are based on many things and not just on recent performance. Many factors such as changes in your income or overall debt, upcoming purchases, job changes, and family life changes can be relevant to your investment portfolio.

Simply put, being "in tune" with changes in your life and how they relate to your investment portfolio and necessary adjustments to it will help ensure that such alterations are based on sound fundamentals and not on short-term events with little impact on your long-term objectives.

Focus on Expenses…But Not Too Much

While expenses play an influential role in underlying performance, sometimes the discussions and opinions of them miss the mark.

Expenses come in the form of many things: 12b-1 fees, management fees, up-front loads, back end loads, trade or transaction costs, and so on. You only need to pick up almost any investment-related trade journal or magazine to see that expenses are on investors' minds and play a big role. It goes without saying that if Fund A has a lower total expense than Fund B and performance over a given time period for each fund is the same; investors in Fund A will have a higher *net* return. From this perspective, expenses will always play a significant role in an investment's rate of return.

However, these types of discussions go beyond the old adage, "Cheaper is better," just as information and easy access to it does not always translate into wise decision-making. In other words, if Fund B is more expensive than Fund A, what are the expenses for it and how do the factors that *make* it more expensive influence return?

So, the sales load takes on a significant meaning when the investment time frame is shorter, where the annual expense ratio is more relevant when the holding period is longer. There is nothing inherently wrong with paying a sales load as long as two important things happen:

- You know how much in fees you are paying
- The amount you are paying is buying you a valuable service

Dividends

The Jobs and Growth Tax Relief Reconciliation Act of 2003 provided a nice benefit for higher-income medical specialists. In years past, investing in companies that pay dividends to shareholders has been somewhat of a tax problem for a physician in a high tax bracket. Dividends were taxed as ordinary income which, for the high-income specialist, translated to a lower rate of return than someone receiving dividend income in a lower tax bracket.

As dividend income can be a very important component of your total return, it is then essential to own such stocks within your overall portfolio.

The Jobs and Growth Tax Relief Reconciliation Act <u>lowered</u> the tax rate for qualified dividends to 15 percent. This tax treatment remains in effect for 2012. For the high-income specialist, this means that instead of keeping less than two-thirds of any dividend income, you will now retain 85 percent!

However, in your planning, it is important to remember that tax laws are subject to change.

Bond and Fixed Income Investments

It is easy to compare the annual average rate of return of stocks versus that of bonds and assume that stocks, with their higher long-term average return, is where the vast majority of your long-term investments should be.

The Capital Accumulation Stage 57

Diversification among asset categories means having exposure to investments that are not correlated. Bond and fixed income investments are influenced by different factors than are stocks, and as such will perform differently in different market cycles. Having exposure to bonds will again lower your portfolio's volatility levels in the short term and make it less likely to commit impulsive short-term investment decisions with your long-term investments.

Dollar Cost Averaging and Portfolio Rebalancing

Some additional strategies to employ when investing include dollar cost averaging and portfolio rebalancing. Dollar cost averaging is the process of investing a fixed amount of money each month (or quarter, or year) without worrying about whether the market is up or down. When it is down, you will buy more shares, bringing your average share price down. Over time, besides the element of forced savings, the tendency to try and outguess the market and purchase shares at the ideal moment are eliminated. Dollar cost averaging does not assure a profit, nor does it protect against loss in declining markets. This investment strategy requires regular investments regardless of the fluctuating price of the investment. You should consider your financial ability to continue investing through periods of low price levels.

When there is a large amount of money to invest, coming up with an investment policy and adhering to it is a must. Once an overall asset allocation mix is chosen based on your goals and objectives, stick to it and change only if there are significant changes in the economy, the portfolio, and/or your goals and objectives. Then, on a regular basis (either quarterly, semiannually, or annually), rebalance the portfolio back to the asset allocation you started with. With this strategy, your investment mix does not get skewed towards more or less risk and volatility. Many current portfolio managers have the capability of providing this rebalancing process on an automatic basis.

A well-balanced portfolio is properly diversified by the following asset decisions:

- Stocks versus bonds
- United States (domestic) investment versus international securities
- Large cap versus small cap stocks
- Growth versus value stocks (Keep this in balance!)
- Short, medium, and long term

There are many good resources to turn to that will help you take this process much further than the scope of this book. We think some of the best information can come from a competent and qualified financial advisor who will listen to you and develop a plan that meets your needs.

In general, a higher investment risk is best for those who:

- can accept short-term losses;
- believe gains will offset losses over the long run;
- will not leave the investment if one or two bad years occur; and
- have a long "investment time horizon."

The best way to learn sound market advice is to listen to the experts. The following quotes from mutual fund leaders all stress the futility of market timing:

Peter Lynch: "My single-most important piece of investment advice is to ignore the short-term fluctuations of the market. From one year to the next, the stock market is a coin flip. It can go up or down. The real money in stocks is made in the third, fourth, and fifth year of your investments, because you are participating in a company's earnings, which grow over time."

Warren Buffet: "I do not have, never have had, and never will have an opinion where the stock market will be a year from now."

Sir John Templeton: "Ignore fluctuations. Do not try to outguess the stock market. Buy a quality portfolio and invest for the long term."

So, to drive it home, invest for the long term and be patient!

The Capital Accumulation Stage

1 Investments in smaller company and micro-cap stocks generally carry a higher level of volatility and risk over the short term.

2. Investment risks associated with international investing, in addition to other risks, include currency fluctuations, political and economic instability and differences in accounting standards.

3. Investment risks associated with investing in the real estate fund/portfolio, in addition to other risks, include rental income fluctuation, depreciation, property tax value changes, and differences in real estate market values.

4. Fixed income securities are subject to credit and interest rate risk and, as such, their value generally will fall as interest rates rise. High yield, lower-rated (junk) bonds generally have greater price swings and higher default risks.

8

The Tax-Advantaged Stage

As a physician, the government likes you! Therefore, the main thrust of this stage is to try and significantly delay, reduce, and/or minimize the impact of taxes on your financial picture. Why? To accumulate and create the highest net worth you possibly can. One method of delaying the tax involves investing dollars into qualified retirement plans. This means the dollars are contributed on a before-tax (qualified) basis. Again, the taxes are not eliminated; they are just deferred until the funds are withdrawn. These plans include individual retirement accounts (IRAs), simplified employee pensions (SEPs), tax-sheltered annuities (TSAs), pension and profit sharing plans, 401k plans, and so on.

The main advantage behind these plans is that the government has given you a significant motivation to save money because your taxable income is reduced dollar for dollar by the contribution, reducing your current tax liability, subject to limitations, depending on your income. In other words, your adjusted gross income is less, which means your taxable income is reduced for the tax year. While these accounts are good places to defer and delay the tax liability during your working years, they present some problems at retirement because of the tax due then. And, transferring qualified assets to heirs can present some tax nightmares if not handled carefully.

The general principal here is to save money into these plans when you are in a higher tax bracket and withdraw the funds at retirement when you are in a lower tax bracket. It must be noted that when you are early in your career or still completing your residency or fellowship, and your income and tax bracket is low, it doesn't make any sense to put a lot of money into an IRA or 401k. Why defer money when you are in the lowest tax bracket you will ever be in? You may want to contribute to a 401k just up to where the employer matches those funds, and then take advantage of the Roth IRA for as long as your income allows you to contribute. Currently, a Roth IRA allows you to contribute up to $5,000 per year on an after-tax basis. They do not provide any tax relief today; the advantage of a Roth IRA is that all investment earnings grow tax-deferred, and provided that certain requirements are met, all distributions after age fifty-nine and a half are withdrawn *tax-free*. (There is a 10% IRS penalty for distributions taken within the first five years or prior to age 59 ½.) So, you are able to forgo the tax break when in a lower tax bracket and withdraw gains tax-free at a time when you may be in a much higher tax environment.

Investors' anticipated tax bracket in retirement will determine whether or not a Roth IRA versus a traditional IRA will provide more money in retirement. Generally, investors who are in a higher tax bracket at retirement relative to their current tax bracket while making contributions to a Roth IRA benefit more than an investor who is in a lower tax bracket at retirement.

Our intention here is not to give an in-depth description of every type of qualified plan available, but rather a brief description of each to help you understand basic terms and definitions associated with each different plan. Highlights of qualified plans include:

- Tax-deductible contributions
- Tax-deferred growth of investment earnings
- Most protected from claims of creditors – Make sure you speak with your attorney.

Some drawbacks of qualified plans include:

- Plan assets are generally illiquid until you reach age 59 ½. (10% IRS penalty applies to distributions prior to age 59 ½.)
- Annual contributions may be restrictive, in particular for the high-income medical specialist.
- All distributions are taxed at ordinary income.
- Complexity of plan design, set up, and administration can be high.

The Tax-Advantaged Stage

Here is a brief discussion of the various retirement plans.

SIMPLE IRAs

A SIMPLE IRA is generally a good option for a practice with a small number of employees. A SIMPLE IRA allows all employees to contribute a portion of their salary each paycheck, and will also require that an employer contribution be made on behalf of all eligible employees. Current guidelines allow each employee to set aside up to $11,500 ($14,000 if age 50 or over) in 2011. Contributions made to the plan will be 100 percent tax deductible. In addition, the employer or practice owner must *either* match employee contributions dollar for dollar up to 3 percent of an employee's compensation *or* make a contribution of 2 percent of compensation for all eligible employees, regardless of whether they are contributing their own money to the plan. SIMPLE IRAs are easy to set up, very inexpensive to administer, and very attractive for smaller medical practices looking to offer a qualified retirement plan without a lot of cost or hassle.

401k Plans

With a 401k plan, employees of the practice may choose to defer up to $16,500 ($22,000 if age 50 or over) annually into the plan on a pre-tax basis. In 2012, this increases to $17,000. In addition, the employer may elect to contribute a portion into the individual employee's account. If you had a 401(k) with a 3 percent match, assuming $160,000 income, the total funding could be $21,300 ($16,500 + [$160,000 × 3 percent] = $21,300). The practice may place a vesting schedule on the matching contributions. The physician/employee would be required to remain with the group a certain number of years for the matching contribution to "vest." A summary of 401k plan benefits include:

- High contribution limits for employer and employees
- A competitive plan to attract and retain key people
- Loan provisions for hardships and emergencies
- Flexibility with respect to matching contributions

A 401k plan has some similar characteristics to a SIMPLE IRA, but they have higher administrative costs and can vary significantly in their complexity. A very common problem with 401k plans is varying levels of employee deferral rates. If the higher paid physicians contribute a significantly higher percentage of their income compared to lower paid employees, the plan may be considered "top-heavy." This means too much money is in the accounts of the higher paid physicians and will restrict the amount of money the physician is able to defer into the plan. This problem can be addressed by adopting a Safe Harbor 401k plan.

Safe Harbor 401k Plans

A safe harbor 401k plan is intended to encourage plan participation among all employees and ease the administrative burden by eliminating IRS tests normally required with a traditional 401k plan. A safe harbor 401k plan allows employees to contribute a percentage of their pay into the plan. It then requires an employer contribution of 3% of compensation on behalf of all eligible employees whether they are participating in the plan or not. This contribution is also always immediately vested. Alternatively, another way to qualify as a safe harbor 401k would be to match 100 percent of participant contributions up to 3 percent of pay, plus an additional 50 percent of participant contributions up to the next 2 percent of pay.

Such plans are ideal for the medical practice with highly compensated specialists whose contribution levels would be restricted with the traditional 401k plan. A safe harbor 401k may be a good fit for a medical practice that:

- Expects low participation by non-highly compensated employees
- Desires the highest limits for employee contributions
- Has very predictable and consistent cash flow to make the mandatory contribution each year
- Wants to eliminate the cost and burden of IRS testing
- Wants lower administrative expense than traditional 401ks

Roth 401k

A Roth 401k is a new type of retirement plan that combines the tax treatment of a Roth IRA with annual contribution limits of a traditional 401k. A medical specialist may opt to take advantage of the Roth 401k if currently in a lower tax environment today than you likely will be in retirement. Such a plan allows you to contribute up to $16,500 annually on an after-tax basis. In other words, there is no tax benefit today associated with the contributions. However, the plan assets grow 100 percent tax-deferred and, provided certain requirements are met, all plan assets are withdrawn on a tax-free basis after age fifty-nine and a half.

A younger medical specialist may be wise to opt for the Roth 401k for the first years after entering private practice when income and tax brackets are likely lower, and switch to the traditional 401k plan when income and associated tax levels increase significantly.

Profit Sharing Plans

Profit sharing plans are designed to allow the employer to contribute to the plan on a discretionary basis. Depending on the terms of the plan, there is no set amount an employer needs to contribute each year. If contributions are made, you must have a set formula for determining how the contributions are allocated among all eligible plan participants. The maximum combined contribution limit the employer can deduct is 25 percent of total eligible payroll (maximum income per employee for consideration in 2011 is $245,000). The maximum amount that can be allocated to the employee's account is 100 percent of total annual pay, or $49,000 in 2011, whichever is less. (This increases to $50,000 in 2012). There are no employee deferrals allowed without adding a 401k feature.

With a profit sharing plan, the main benefit to the practice owner is the flexible nature of the contributions. It is possible to adjust contributions each year, depending on profitability of the clinic, as long as contributions are frequent and ongoing. A real, tangible benefit of a profit sharing plan for the employee is having contributions to the plan tied to the performance and overall profitability of the clinic.

Money Purchase Plans

A money purchase plan is very similar to a profit sharing plan in terms of contribution limits, benefits to employer and employee, setup and ongoing administrative costs, and eligibility. The primary difference is that employer contribution is a plan requirement. This amount is stated in the plan document. The benefit of a money purchase plan for the employer is the fixed annual contributions to the plan make it easier to budget for and offers a measure of comfort and predictability for the employee. The inflexibility is often a big enough drawback that most practices gravitate to the other choices. It is beyond the scope of this text, but for certain situations (i.e., a small number of employees with one or two older and highly paid specialists), a money purchase plan and/or a variation of it can provide for sizable annual deferral limits that exceed the other plans. Consult with a financial planner and tax advisor who specialize in working with high-income physicians to work with you on this decision.

Simplified Employee Pensions (SEP IRAs)

A SEP IRA is a retirement plan that looks much like a profit sharing plan. The contribution limit is 25 percent of employee compensation up to a maximum of $49,000 in 2011. ($50,000 in 2012). The administrative costs associated with a SEP IRA are very minimal, as are reporting and tax filing requirements. The plan must cover all employees who have worked for the group in three of the past five years and are twenty-one years or older. SEP IRA plans are attractive for medical groups that have unpredictable cash flow, as contributions to the plan can vary or not be made at all, depending on profitability. The contributions are 100 percent employer-paid with no employee contributions allowed.

SEP IRAs can also be particularly attractive for the medical specialist that has additional self-employment income from moonlighting. Contributions for self-employment income are based on net income, minus 50 percent of self-employment taxes paid and any deductible plan contributions or a maximum of $49,000. Since self-employment income is taxed very heavily, such a plan can be a very effective tool to lessen the tax burden. In addition, SEP plans may provide creditor protection at both the federal and state level. Make sure to discuss this with your attorney.

The Tax-Advantaged Stage

In summary, qualified plans are an integral part of your retirement, and there are many ways in which you can design a plan. When your income is at the highest tax bracket, we generally advocate taking full advantage of the plan available to you through your employer and contributing the maximum annual contribution limit allowable under current tax law. If you are either joining a newer practice or starting your own practice and have questions or concerns regarding the existing plan or a new plan, we encourage you to contact a competent financial advisor for several reasons:

- Your qualified plan will likely be your largest retirement asset, and as such should be carefully invested and monitored.
- Tax laws surrounding such plans have changed considerably and continue to change each year. This requires more time on your part to ensure that you have the most appropriate plan that provides you maximum benefit given your circumstances.
- Tax arbitrage planning opportunities exist. You should invest in a qualified plan at a high tax bracket and withdraw the funds at a lower bracket. So, your retirement income will likely come from several sources as you design a retirement income strategy to maximize your after-tax income.

Calculating Your Tax Bracket

Just for you, we have taken the 10,000-page tax code and narrowed it down to two pages. (See pages 70-71.) Wouldn't it be nice if preparing our taxes was this easy! This is, of course, a basic guide only, just for education purposes, and doesn't factor in some of the specifics such as child care, student loan interest deductions, moving expenses, and so on. But, surprisingly, this is fairly accurate in estimating the federal tax liability.

We encourage working with your accountant or running one of the tax software packages any time you have a major change in your life that will affect your taxes. As a helpful approximation, the guide here should provide a good planning estimate. Family changes such as a birth, death, or marriage all affect the tax you owe. Financial changes such as a new job, a raise, going back to school, and buying or moving to a new house will also impact your tax liability, and a new calculation should be made. Compare your calculation to the amount you are having withheld from your paycheck, and if you are withholding too much, change this with your employer by filling out a new W-4 form.

This is especially useful for most everyone whose incomes adjust in accordance with their training. In July or August, you may start your employment and/or have a scheduled increase in your income or become a partner. If you don't work with your employer on the correct tax withholding, they will take out an amount that would correspond to you working for the whole year. Generally, there are many expenses and having a higher take-home pay would most likely be more beneficial than getting a tax refund the following spring.

There are some important basic points to understand about taxes. First, getting a large refund isn't really all that smart. It means you just gave the government an interest-free loan for the year. If you are a terrible saver and use this as a forced savings plan, we're guessing it still backfires on you because you know the lump sum tax refund is coming and you have plans for spending that amount, too! In any event, we suggest that you estimate your tax liability in advance and try to end up about even. That avoids any under-withholding penalties and any unexpected tax liability due that you may not be prepared for.

The second point is that it is always in your best interest to make more money! We've heard people say, "I just got a raise and it jumped me into the next tax bracket, so I'm going to take home less!" That's not how it works. The tax system is a progressive tax, and the more income you make, the more you take home. It's just that each additional dollar is taxed at a higher percentage, but the first dollars are taxed the same. Repeated, moving into a higher tax bracket affects the last of your dollars you earn, but the first dollars are still taxed at the same rate.

As an example, let's look at the Basic Federal Tax Estimator on the next few pages. Plug in your income (wages, interest income, etc.) and subtract contributions to pretax accounts to get your adjusted gross income. From that, subtract your personal exemptions and either the standard deduction or your itemized deductions, whichever is higher. Then look up your tax bracket on the chart. The tax bracket is the tax on each additional dollar

The Tax-Advantaged Stage

you earn, or the tax that is saved by virtue of reducing your taxable income by $1.

Suppose you are married and your taxable income happens to be $212,300. Your neighbor's taxable income comes in at $212,301, or $1 more. Bummer for them, right? Yes and no. Their tax liability is only 33 cents more than yours, because each new dollar is taxed at the 33 percent rate. They still have a take-home pay of 67 cents more than you, so while at a higher tax bracket, their take-home pay is more.

Your total tax is calculated as follows:

	The tax is:
First $17,000 of taxable income:	$1,700 (17,000 × .1)
$17,000 to $69,000 of taxable income:	$7,800 (52,000 × .15)
$69,000 to $139,350 of taxable income:	$17,587.5 (70,350 × .25)
$139,350 to $212,300 of taxable income:	$20,426 (72,950 × .28)
Remainder of income up to $225,000:	$4,191 (12,700 × .33)
Total Federal Tax:	**$51,704.5**

Your friend's tax bill would be calculated the same as yours with another 33 cents of tax liability on the $1 above $212,300 at the 33 percent tax bracket. Work through your own situation a few times and this should be easier to understand.

Basic Federal Tax Estimator

This is a guide only and is current as of 2011. For the most current tax law information, see www.basictaxestimator.com. This does not factor in child care, student loan interest deductions, medical expenses, moving, and so on.

Gross Income: Wages, Interest Income, etc.

_____

Minus: **Adjustments:** IRA, 401(k), TSA, etc.

_____
=
Equals: **Adjusted Gross Income (AGI)**

_____

Minus:

    Personal Exemptions ($3,700 × # in household)
    (Phased out as income exceeds certain limits)

_____

And the higher of:
    Standard Deduction
    (Single: $5,800; Married: $11,600)

_____

Or

    Itemized Deductions

        ☐ State Income and/or Local Taxes

        ☐ Home Mortgage Interest and Property Tax

The Tax-Advantaged Stage

☐ Charitable Contributions

Equals: **Taxable Income**   =

Federal Income Tax Due: (See tax table below.)

2011 Individual Income Tax Rates

Single				Married Filing Jointly			
$0	to	$8,500	10%	$0	to	$17,000	10%
$8,501	to	$34,500	15%	$17,001	to	$69,000	15%
$34,501	to	$83,600	25%	$69,001	to	$139,350	25%
$83,601	to	$174,400	28%	$139,351	to	$212,300	28%
$174,401	to	$379,150	33%	$212,301	to	$379,150	33%
$379,151	+	No limit	35%	$379,151	+	No Limit	35%

What Do You Do At Retirement?

Estimating your retirement needs is an important factor to consider at this stage of the pyramid. A financial planning rule of thumb is to figure on needing 70 to 80 percent of your pre-retirement income, although more and more people are enjoying a retirement lifestyle that is close to their working years. This figure should be based on the income you plan to be earning at retirement, not that which you're making today. To estimate this, look at your current expenses and subtract the expenses and savings that will not be needed at retirement, and add in extra expenses (i.e., travel, medical, etc.) that may be needed then. Consider the following:

- Will you still be paying a mortgage?
- Do you anticipate hefty medical expenses for yourself or a spouse?
- Do you wish to travel extensively?
- Will your day-to-day living expenses be similar to or less than what they are now?

If your budget allows and you have your *Security and Confidence Stage* taken care of, then take full advantage of any 401k or similar plans your employer offers, at least up until the amount the employer matches. This type of retirement investment defers tax payment on the contributed earnings until the money is withdrawn, usually at retirement. If your employer matches any of your contribution, this is an added tax benefit.

Universal Retirement Truths

Over the years, as retirement planning has become increasingly complicated, there are four simple "truths" behind any advice we offer on retirement planning, no matter how complicated the specific issue.

Start Early

The sooner you begin contributing to your retirement plan, the more time your money has to compound. You can always make adjustments to keep your investment allocation on track with your risk tolerance and time horizon profile. However, if you delay getting started entirely, it is very difficult to catch up.

Diversify

With regard to your retirement plan, after you have determined an appropriate investment allocation for your contributions, make sure you understand the investment objectives of each individual fund you are investing in.

Two funds with different names may have very similar investment objectives as well as holdings. Deferring into each fund will not give you the same degree of diversification as investing in two funds with different objectives.

We recommend you work with a financial professional to determine an appropriate asset allocation for your retirement assets and make sure you achieve a high level of diversification among the investment options.

Invest Consistently

Most plans allow for contributions to be made on a payroll deduction basis. This allows for contributions to be made to your investments each and

The Tax-Advantaged Stage

every month. This eliminates any tendency to "time" the market and over time, consistent investing can help you lower your investments costs. Regular investing over time is a proven method that "forces" you to buy more shares when the price of a fund is down and fewer when prices are higher.

Dollar cost averaging will produce a lower average cost per share compared to the average price per share over time.

Hang Tough

If your retirement is still fifteen, twenty, even thirty years away, generally speaking, if you want the highest return potential, you should heavily consider constructing a more aggressive investment allocation than that of an investment objective with a shorter time horizon. It is perfectly natural that such an investment allocation will experience higher levels of short-term fluctuation. This is necessary to potentially achieve a higher long-term rate of return.

As the time when you will begin drawing on this money draws nearer, it will be necessary to begin shifting a greater percentage of your assets towards investments geared more towards capital preservation. The time to worry about this is not during your peak earning years when retirement is still many years away. Ideally, at retirement, you have multiple income sources and are withdrawing money from your qualified plans to "fill up" your 25 percent bracket and supplementing that with withdrawals from your non-qualified funds and variable life policies for maximum tax leverage and efficiency. This is an area where the advice and wisdom of an experienced financial planner will be very valuable.

Life insurance products contain fees, such as mortality and expense charges, and may contain restrictions, such as surrender charges.

Policy loans and withdrawals may create an adverse tax result in the event of a lapse or policy surrender, and will reduce both the cash value and death benefit.

Please keep in mind that the primary reason to purchase a life insurance product is the death benefit.

9

529 College Savings Plans

When it comes to planning for your children's future education costs, 529 College Savings Plans can provide a great tax-advantaged investment opportunity for the high-income medical specialist. From an investment standpoint, such plans enjoy tax-deferred growth of earnings, extremely generous contribution limits, and currently tax-free distributions of investment gains for all qualified education expenses. (We'll expand on qualified expenses in a moment.)

It is our opinion that the features that make such plans so attractive have less to do with their tax treatment and more to do with issues of control and flexibility.

Let's look at these plans from two difference perspectives:

- Investment and tax features
- Control and flexibility features

Tax and Investment Features

For the high-income medical specialist, one frustrating aspect of investment planning from a tax perspective is that, when income increases beyond certain annual amounts, many investments that have attractive tax treatment become unavailable (Roth IRAs) or annual contribution limits become more restrictive as income goes up (401k plans). Neither of these is an issue with the 529 Plan. All investment earnings on the plan grow 100 percent tax-deferred, and the contribution limits are such that they would rarely be restrictive for the purpose of funding a child's education.

Contributions

Contributions to 529 plans are not tax-deductible but are considered gifts for federal and estate tax purposes. For the 2011 tax year, anyone may take advantage of the annual gift tax exclusion by contributing $13,000 per year ($26,000 for married couples) to any beneficiary. For financially independent physicians, there is a very unique rule for 529 Plans that allows for an individual to utilize five years worth of annual gift tax exclusion by contributing up to $65,000 ($130,000 for married couples) in one calendar year.

This is a very nice feature for the high net worth specialist looking for ways to incorporate gifting strategies into their estate plan.

The limits imposed on 529 Plans are, generally speaking, so high that it is difficult to envision a scenario where it would become restrictive. The total limits outside of the above discussed annual limits do vary a bit from state to state. They are in the neighborhood of $280,000 to $320,000 per beneficiary! Provided you get started early on planning for your children or grandchildren's future education costs to take full advantage of the tax-deferred growth of investment earnings, such limits should not present a problem.

Distributions

Money has been contributed to a 529 Plan for the benefit of a child or grandchild, and the plan balance has grown significantly over the years. Now it is time to begin withdrawing the money to pay for college expenses, so what happens? When money is withdrawn from the account, it will be considered one of two things: a qualified distribution or a non-qualified distribution.

- Distributions that are utilized to pay for qualified expenses such as room, board, tuition, and certain expenses will be considered qualified withdrawals, and as such are free of both federal and, currently, state income tax. For the physician with a long time horizon and children bound for academic greatness (and the accompanying price tag), there is potential to build up and withdraw all investment gains free of tax!

- Distributions that are utilized for anything other than a qualified expense will be considered a non-qualified distribution. The investment earnings will be taxed as ordinary income for the beneficiary and subject to a 10 percent penalty. As this book is written with the high-income medical specialist in mind, we consider the potential of having investment earnings of a child's 529 Plan *potentially* taxed at the *child's* rate plus a penalty, a worthwhile risk to take.

It should be noted that with many state plans there is a tax deduction for contributions to the state plan where you hold your primary residence. Because each state varies and the laws are changing, consult with a tax advisor who is familiar with the rules in your state.

Control and Flexibility Features

The tax and investment features of IRC Section 529 College Plans are undeniably attractive and make such plans a very powerful financial tool for the high-income medical specialist. However, given the uncertainty of a young child's academic future, we often find reluctance among our clients to fund such vehicles for your child, who may or may not need the money. These uncertainties are very well addressed in 529 plans.

Let's look at some of their benefits from a control and flexibility standpoint.

Who controls the account? The account owner controls the account. If your child reaches the age of majority in your home state, the 529 Plan balance does not become an asset of your child! You, as account owner, control how and when distributions are to be made.

Who can contribute to the account? Anyone may make contributions to the plan.

What happens if my child receives a scholarship or goes to a less expensive school? Perhaps one of the most attractive features of 529 Plans from a flexibility standpoint is the ability to change beneficiaries at any point. However, in order to avoid triggering penalty on investment earnings, the new beneficiary must be a family member of the previous beneficiary. The ability to move money in one designated 529 Plan to another child's plan, should he or she not go to school, attend a less expensive school, receive a scholarship, or any other reason, is a unique feature that gives parents a great deal of flexibility.

What happens if money is not used for college? If the money being withdrawn from a 529 Plan is being used for anything other than a qualified higher education expense, the investment earnings will be taxed at the beneficiaries' tax rate, plus a 10 percent penalty on earnings. Pulling money out of 529 Plans for non-qualified expenses should be avoided. However, as the earnings are taxed at the beneficiaries' rate, it is not too terrible as the account has grown completely tax-deferred!

Must the beneficiary go to school in the state whose plan I used? No. Currently, all states recognize other state-sponsored 529 Plans, and as such, all distributions for qualified expenses will be both federally and state tax-exempt.

Funding Your Child's IRC Section 529 College Savings Plan

With all the advantages of 529 Plans, the obvious question becomes, "How do we fund a plan for our child?"

When determining how to take full advantage of such plans, there are several assumptions you can predict with a fairly high degree of accuracy. Such factors include:

- Year in which your child enters college.
- How many years (four or five) of post-secondary education you wish to be able to fund.
- The percentage of the total cost you as a parent wish to be able to pay for.

There are also many more variables you must simply make a best estimate for. A few of these factors include:

- The rate of inflation for college costs. College costs have experienced significant levels of increase over the years and will likely continue to rise at a greater rate than the overall cost of living.
- The investment rate of return of the assets in the 529 Plan.
- Where your child will attend school.

All of these variables must be considered when determining how to fund your child's plan to arrive at the most important objective: having adequate funds available within the plan to be able to pay for the type of education, the length of education, and the location of the education you planned for. Any outcome other than this will result in one of two scenarios:

- Not enough money saved up in the 529 Plan. This will likely result in funds being withdrawn from other investment vehicles that have not grown tax-deferred and will likely not enjoy the tax benefits when withdrawn. As qualified distributions will be both state and federally tax-exempt, investment gains from other sources will likely be subject to tax! As discussed earlier, this is where an over-funded variable life insurance policy can come in very handy. Please see page 49 for important information regarding life insurance.
- Too much money saved up in the 529 Plan. The likely result of too much money in the plan will be excessive non-qualified distributions. While the earnings will be taxed at your child's rate and thus at a lower rate, this is only in the event that it is withdrawn for the benefit of the beneficiary. Should the money *not* be withdrawn for the benefit of your child, all investment earnings will taxed at *your* ordinary income rate plus a 10 percent penalty! So, err on the conservative side and fund a 529 Plan at a level you feel comfortable with.

Our conclusion is that 529 College Savings Plans are excellent financial tools for the purpose of saving for future college costs. They are particularly attractive for the high-income medical specialist, given their investment, tax, and flexibility features. Like all aspects of your financial planning, regular monitoring is critical. As your child's academic greatness (hopefully!) begins to materialize, adjusting the contributions to the plan accordingly will ensure that the many benefits can be maximized.

A 529 Plan is a tax-advantaged investment program designed to help pay for qualified education costs. Participation in a 529 Plan does not guarantee that the contributions and investment returns will be adequate to cover higher education expenses. Contributors to the plan assume all investment risk, including the potential for loss of principal and any penalties for non-educational withdrawals.

Your state of residence may offer state tax advantages to residents who participate in the in-state plan. You may miss out on certain state tax advantages, should you choose another state's 529 Plan. Any state-based benefits should be one of many appropriately weighted factors to be considered in making an investment decision. You should consult your financial, tax, or other advisor to learn more about how state-based benefits (including any limitations) would apply to your specific circumstances. You may also wish to contact your home state's 529 Plan program administrator to learn more about the benefits that might be available to you by investing in the in-state plan.

[1] It should be noted that with many state plans there is a tax deduction for contributions to the state plan where you hold your primary residence. Because each state varies and the laws are changing, consult with a tax advisor who is familiar with the rules in your state.

10

The Speculation Stage

The *Speculation Stage* involves risking money you can afford to lose. Some people are never comfortable with this and thus should not consider it. These people should simply build their financial pyramid wider. This stage can involve different things for different people. It could be buying very speculative individual stocks or aggressive specialty mutual funds.

Subjecting your money where the principal has a high degree of volatility and risk has potentially high returns, but your money could also be lost completely. It is appropriate that this stage fits at the top of the pyramid because if the money is lost, it won't be devastating to your overall financial plan.

Our rule of thumb when deciding how much to risk in a business opportunity or other aggressive venture is one year's worth of net worth growth. Never invest more than this! In a worst case scenario, if you lost the entire amount of your investment, you have basically lost one year's worth of financial progress. While not fun, it is not financially devastating. People get into trouble and can't recover financially when they take a lifetime's worth of savings and gamble with it.

As an example, let's say your net worth is $1,000,000 and conservatively projected a year from now, it will be $1,080,000. This growth would be from additional savings, reducing debts, and/or growth from your existing assets. In any event, the $80,000 projected growth is the absolute maximum amount that could be considered for a very speculative investment.

In the event that an opportunity has come along that requires more than this amount, do not be tempted to risk more. Consider lowering your investment, delaying the timing until your net worth has grown, or involving a financial partner.

Again, keep in mind, speculative investments, while valid financial tools, are typically used only by extremely savvy investors, and/or high net worth investors and institutions. They are not recommended to anyone who cannot afford to lose a substantial amount of their net worth. These investments carry an extraordinary amount of risk, and generally require intensive research and knowledge to carry out the investment.

In summary, no one has ever gotten into trouble financially by being too conservative for too long. Sure, there are some potential lost opportunity costs, but you can get into a lot of financial trouble by being too aggressive with too much money. That's why the financial pyramid is such a useful tool to help organize and prioritize these decisions.

11

Estate Planning with Asset Protection Strategies

This chapter was written by Robert Kaufer, an Attorney with Kaufer Law Firm, LLC. and has been included for educational purposes only. The applicability of many of the strategies discussed may be dependent upon the specific laws of states or countries in which the strategies are carried out. Financial Advisors do not provide specific tax or legal advice and this information should not be considered as such. You should always consult your tax and/or legal advisor regarding your own specific situation.

Asset protection planning should not be viewed as a strategy to avoid paying legitimate and reasonable creditors, but as a process to protect your personal assets from unreasonable creditors. "Unreasonable creditors" are those who bring frivolous lawsuits or get unreasonable jury awards related to medical malpractice or personal liability claims such as automobile or slip-and-fall accidents. These unreasonable creditors do exist. They are the predators looking to sue anyone who is successful. It could be any legal action where a valid claim simply doesn't exist.

In general, "asset protection" is about putting up barriers in front of the unreasonable creditors to make it difficult or impossible for them to get your personal and business assets. The key questions are:

1. What should I do?
2. When should I do it?
3. How far do I need to go?

What Should I Do?

The first step in navigating through the asset protection choices is to get educated. This chapter is not intended to be an exhaustive treatise on asset protection, but a primer to get you going in the right direction. It also is not intended to be legal advice and should not be taken as such. It is for information purposes only. Before implementing any asset protection strategy, you should consult with an attorney licensed to practice law in your state.

Exempt Assets

The first line of defense against unreasonable creditors is the protection you get from the state you live in. Each state, through its statutes, exempts certain assets from creditors. These assets can include all or a portion of the following:

- *Home:* In many states, you get an exemption from creditors for your home. This, however, is usually not an unlimited exemption, and in some states (New Jersey, for example) there is no exemption at all. Other states (such as Florida) give an unlimited exemption, meaning a creditor cannot force you to sell your home to pay off a judgment no matter what the value is. While these two states present both ends of the spectrum, the bulk of the states fall somewhere in between. An example is Minnesota, where the statute allows you to protect $200,000 of equity in your home. If the difference between your home's market value and all mortgages is greater than $200,000, a creditor can force you to sell your home, paying to the creditor any amount over the exemption.

- *Life insurance:* Some states will protect life insurance partially or entirely. This can be both the cash value and/or death benefit.
    - Some states such as Arizona, Florida, Illinois, Indiana, Kentucky, Massachusetts, Ohio, and Texas protect the cash value paid into a life insurance contract. As long as certain conditions under each state's laws are met, a

Estate Planning with Asset Protection Strategies

creditor cannot use a judgement to force the withdrawal of funds to pay off a debt.
- To contrast the laws of the above states, Minnesota only protects death benefits of $20,000 if paid to the surviving spouse or child and cash value of $4,000. Any amount above these can be reached by a creditor. Check with your local attorney in the event that this has changed.

- *Annuities:* Annuities are similar to life insurance. Each state decides how much, if any, can be protected from creditors.

- *IRAs:* IRAs are also given a certain amount of protection by state laws, and the protection varies from state to state. Again, it can be all, nothing, or somewhere in between. The trend, however, is for greater protection to be given to these types of accounts. You should stay tuned as these laws are changing, as you can see by Congress recently passing new bankruptcy legislation that included provisions for increased protection of Traditional and Roth IRAs owned by a person in a bankruptcy proceeding.

- *ERISA-governed retirement plans:* These plans are most commonly employer-sponsored profit-sharing/401(k) plans. They are different from IRAs in that they are governed by federal law instead of state law. In most cases, federal law will trump state laws, including judgments that require an ERISA-governed plan to liquidate assets to pay a creditor.

An attorney licensed in your state should be contacted to determine what protections your state will give you against the unreasonable creditor.

Basic Estate Planning: Wills or Revocable Trusts

The foundation for any asset protection strategy is to have your basic estate plan in place. The two primary documents you can choose from for your basic estate plan are the will or the revocable living trust. While neither of these estate planning documents give much asset protection during your life, they can (if properly drafted) give good protection to your heirs.

The Will

Having a will does not avoid probate. It is an instruction manual to the probate court on how your probate-eligible property should be distributed, who should do it, and, if your children are under the age of majority, who should be their guardian. While you are alive, it does nothing to give you asset protection as you continue to own your property in your name. It may give some asset protection to your heirs, depending on the complexity of the planning.

The probate process is designed to be a creditor's forum. Any known creditors must be given notice, and there is a waiting period for creditors to stake their claim.

The Revocable Living Trust

A revocable living trust is an alternative to using a will for your primary estate planning documents. Having a properly funded revocable living trust will avoid probate. While it will avoid the probate process, it offers limited protection of your assets from creditors. It can, however, if correctly drafted, give good asset protection for your heirs after your death.

The fact that the revocable living trust, if properly funded, avoids the probate process and the creditor-friendly rules that come with it, is reason enough to choose them over wills for your basic estate planning vehicles.

Family Limited Liability Companies and Family Limited Partnerships

One of the more common strategies used in asset protection to build upon the basic estate planning is the (family) limited liability company (FLLC) or (family) limited partnership (FLP).

FLLC

An LLC is a new form of business entity that has become increasingly popular. It combines the liability protection of a corporation with the tax and asset protection advantages of a general partnership. All fifty states have enacted LLC laws, with most of them looking and feeling like a general partnership. Some states (Minnesota, in particular) have taken on the feel of the corporation with the two levels of management (governor and manager). This feature makes it ideal for the family LLC, because it allows husband and wife to maintain various levels of control over the company, depending on their life circumstances.

An LLC can elect to be taxed like a corporation **or** a partnership. However, the majority of LLCs today elect to be taxed like a partnership. That means these LLCs do not pay income tax. The income flows through directly to the members and is reported on their personal tax returns.

To begin the LLC, articles of organization are filed with the state in which you intend to set up the company. Some states (such as Minnesota) allow you to keep the names of the members, governors, and managers private, with only the name of the organizer being filed (in most cases, the attorney who sets up the company). Having this anonymity can provide for benefits and is an important component of an asset protection strategy.

FLP

ABSol Partnerships
General Partnerships

A general partnership is formed when two or more people agree to carry on a business together to make a profit. It is as simple as that, and no writing has to be made and no documents need to be filed with the state except for registering the name to be used. It is good practice, however, for any partnership to have a written partnership agreement so all partners understand their rights and responsibilities. The problem with a general partnership is that all partners are jointly and separately liable for all debts of the partnership. The general partnership should be avoided at all costs because of this liability trap. If a partnership is to be used in an asset protection setting, it should be formed as a limited partnership.

Limited Partnerships

A limited partnership consists of one or more general partners and one or more limited partners. A general partner handles the control and management of the partnership. The tradeoff for this is that he or she has unlimited personal liability for all debts and obligations of the partnership. The limited partners cannot be involved in the control or management of the partnership, but they do enjoy protection from the debts of the partnership because their liability is limited to their investments in the entity. If a limited partner does participate in the control or management of the partnership, they may lose their limited liability.

Certain business formalities must be followed to help ensure limited liability protection.

Choosing Between the Two

For many years, the FLP was the entity of choice for asset protection and the minimization of estate taxes, but since its advent, the LLC is fast becoming the entity of choice because it is more flexible than the FLP and because there is no unlimited liability for the general partners as there is with an FLP. In an FLLC, the husband and wife can be involved in the management of the company without losing their liability shield while there are no creditors. If a lawsuit arises, the spouse/defendant resigns from their management role but retains their personal liability protection (limited liability assets used in entity).

Creditors Cannot Reach Assets of an FLP or FLLC

In most states, the only remedy for a judgment creditor of an LLC or FLP is a "charging order." A charging order is a legal remedy that gives the creditor the right to receive any distributions from an FLP or FLLC. It does not give the creditor the right to become an owner or to have a say in the management of the company. The creditor only receives the distributions intended to go to the owner/debtor. If this happens, the FLP/FLLC will simply choose not to make any distributions. The poison pill, however, is that even if the FLP or FLLC does not make a distribution, the creditor is responsible for the tax consequences as if a distribution had been made when the entity is taxed as a partnership.

The idea behind charging order protection is simple enough. Owners should not be involuntarily forced into a partnership with somebody they

Estate Planning with Asset Protection Strategies

do not choose. To get complete protection from this strategy, however, great care must be put into the operating agreement to give the maximum protection possible from creditors. Using this entity to hold the assets you most want to protect allows you to protect them from creditors.

Trusts

Irrevocable Trusts

In planning, it is important to keep the revocable living trust concept talked about separate from the irrevocable trust. The revocable living trust can be amended or revoked (you retain complete control as long as you are alive and competent), but it gives limited asset protection. On the other hand, the irrevocable trust will protect your assets (assuming the transfer of property was not a fraudulent conveyance), but you lose all control and benefit. In a properly executed asset protection strategy, they do play an important role.

One of the more common uses is to own life insurance. If the trust is created properly and all of the administrative formalities are followed, it will keep the proceeds out of a deceased person's estate for tax purposes and keep them away from creditors.

Asset Protection Trusts

A strategy that is gaining popularity is the asset protection trust (APT). An APT is a self-settled trust, meaning it is funded by the creator of the trust, who is also the beneficiary. This is different from the irrevocable trust discussed above, because in a traditional irrevocable trust, the intended beneficiary is usually the spouse or children and not the person who creates the trust.

There are two main types of APTs: the domestic APT and the offshore (foreign) APT.

Domestic APT

In many states, the self-settled APT is not allowed. But in a minority of states, recent legislation is beginning to allow such asset protection vehicles. Eight states (Alaska, Delaware, Rhode Island, Missouri, Utah, Oklahoma, South Dakota, and Nevada) now allow some form of a self-settled trust to be set up that is outside the reach of creditors. These are very new and have yet to be challenged in court. Many legal scholars believe they are unconstitutional because of the "Full Faith and Credit" clause of the U.S. Constitution, which says, "A state is to recognize the judgment from another state." This sets up a conflict of state laws issue (the self-settled APT is exempt from judgment creditors in the state it was created) and the U.S. Constitution. This means the creditor must simply register the judgment and does not have to initiate the lawsuit over again in that state.

Until the above-mentioned conflict of laws issue is settled in court, the domestic APT should probably be avoided unless you happen to live in one of the states where they are recognized. These trusts are usually expensive to set up and administer, and they are probably not a good choice for asset protection unless you are a citizen of a state that has enacted the legislation.

Offshore APT

An offshore or foreign APT is similar to the domestic APT except the trust *situs* (location) is in a foreign jurisdiction. The Cook Islands and Nevis are two popular destinations. These trusts are self-settled, but the trustee is located in one of these foreign jurisdictions, thereby putting them out of reach of the U.S. courts. A creditor would not simply be able to register a U.S. judgment in one of these jurisdictions. They would have to initiate a new lawsuit.

While the trustee and trust may be outside the reach of the U.S. courts, the creator of the trust is not outside that reach unless he or she leaves the country. Many state and federal judges despise this setup and will do whatever is in their power to unwind this type of trust, including putting the creator of the trust in jail for contempt of court. There is a long line of cases that deal with this issue, many not favorable to the debtor. These trusts are also very expensive to set up and administer, and should probably only be used in extreme cases and not with all assets. Consult with an expert asset protection attorney before considering these trusts.

When Should I Do It?

Time should be used as an ally. Having a plan in place and implemented for a period of time before an event (judgment or death) occurs will give the plan a better chance of withstanding an attack by a creditor or the Internal Revenue Service. If you wait until a lawsuit is initiated or even after an event occurs that may cause a lawsuit to be initiated, it may be too late because any transfer may be deemed a "fraudulent conveyance" and will likely quash any asset protection strategies you implement, on the theory that their only purpose was to deny creditors their claims.

How Far Do I Need to Go?

You need to take the steps necessary to give you and your family a sense of security. Assess your risk with the cost of implementing an asset protection plan, and take the action that gives you the protection you're comfortable with. With that in mind, here are some planning rules of thumb.

Planning Rules of Thumb

The following rules of thumb are a guide to assist the physician in deciding what they should do for asset protection. However, the final decisions must weigh the risk of a lawsuit with the cost of the protection. In many cases, the tools referenced in this chapter make good sense for the physician, no matter the stage of his or her career.

1. *In medical school without children:* You may not need to undertake any estate planning at this time, but you should consult with an attorney in your area to make the final decision.
2. *In medical school with children:* If you have children, you need to take some action to get the bare minimum for estate planning. You should be considering guardians for custody of your children and trustees to handle their finances if both parents die. If asset protection concerns or will concern you, you should begin with revocable trusts. Another option is to use testamentary trusts inside

of your will. Keep in mind that these techniques alone do not provide asset protection for you, though they can provide protection to your heirs. These options are more expensive than basic wills, but it will be money well spent, as these will be the foundation of your overall plan.
3. *Residency:* If you are ending your residency, you most likely will have a low net worth and high debt load. Even though your net worth is relatively low, you should consider enlisting an attorney to help you set up revocable trusts with pour-over wills as your main estate planning tools.
4. *In practice:* If you are in practice and asset protection concerns you, you should look to implementing the following procedures if your state-given exemptions do not give you the protection you want and need:
    a. If you have substantial after-tax investments, including cash value life insurance, annuities, rental real estate, or recreational property, you should consider an FLLC.
    b. If you have an FLLC, use it for your cash value life insurance. Then you could use a separate irrevocable life insurance trust for your term insurance with total death benefits greater than $1.5 million to avoid estate taxes and protect the death benefits for your heirs.

Conclusion

If the intended goal of asset protection is to be completely judgment-proof, successful asset protection becomes extremely difficult. However, if the goal is to protect a portion of your estate against the unreasonable creditor, that goal can be obtained with the help of an experienced financial planner and attorney. Without successful asset protection planning, you may lose all assets that are not exempt if you get a judgment awarded against you. With the right planning, you will be able to build walls between you and your creditors that will improve your bargaining position and help you protect what you have worked so hard to earn.

Remember, you need to take action before there are any potential lawsuits against you. Otherwise, any actions taken may be unraveled by the courts.

Estate Planning with Asset Protection Strategies

As with every aspect of a financial plan, the estate planning and asset protection components are extensive and we recommend they be coordinated by a professional advisor working with your tax and legal advisor. The advisor should obviously be very knowledgeable, but also one who listens to you and your goals, and then communicates your options…so you can work together.

You've worked hard to educate yourself in your field. We hope that this book provides you with a framework to begin your financial plan, and that you achieve all of your goals and dreams.

Disclaimers and Other Documents

The U.S. Treasury Department requires us to advise you that to the extent that this message or any attachment concerns tax matters it is not intended or written by our firm to be used, and cannot be used by any taxpayer, for the purpose of avoiding any penalties that may be imposed under the Internal Revenue Code or any other law.

It should be stressed that asset protection is a complicated area of law. Consequently, you should discuss your specific situation with a qualified asset protection attorney.

What Is IRS Circular 230?

The Treasury Department and the Internal Revenue Service have been engaged in an effort to curb abusive tax shelters. As part of this effort, they have issued final regulations under IRS Circular 230 "…to restore, promote, and maintain the public's confidence in those individuals and firms…" who act as tax advisors. It's important to note that we are not tax or legal advisors. You should seek the advice of your own tax and legal advisors regarding any tax and legal issues applicable to your specific circumstance.

This is an explanation of how our correspondence with you (including e-mails) will be affected by new IRS regulations governing tax practitioners. The rules in effect require individuals to add certain standard language to many of our letters, memos, e-mails, and other correspondence concerning federal tax matters that are not meant to be interpreted as specific tax or legal advice. You have probably already seen similar language on written communications from your other correspondence. Although the specific wording may vary depending on the circumstances, you can expect to see notices similar to the following:

IRS Circular 230 Notice:

To the extent that this message or any attachment concerns tax matters it is not intended or written by our firm to be used, and cannot be used by any taxpayer, for the purpose of avoiding any penalties that may be imposed under the Internal Revenue Code or any other law.

The rules require such notices to be "prominently disclosed," i.e., "readily apparent" to the reader. The notice must be in a separate section (but not in a footnote) of the correspondence. Also, "fine-print" notices won't work. The typeface used must be at least the same size as the typeface used in any discussion of facts or law.

A practitioner who fails to satisfy the requirement of the new rules risks censure, disbarment, and substantial penalties.

Please be assured that this policy does not reflect any decrease in the quality of our services or the amount of thought we put into our correspondence with you.

12

Case Studies

Observations and Overview

In this chapter, we provide five specific case studies that demonstrate the concepts outlined in this book. These will show that the pyramid of financial needs can be used in most circumstances as a method of organizing and prioritizing financial decisions. Of course, much of this is subjective, and ultimately the correct answer merges the quantitative and qualitative aspects of the decision into a financial plan you are comfortable with. We hope you find the following case studies to be a very helpful addition to the understanding of the techniques presented earlier in this book.

The following case studies are fictitious, and any similarities to any actual person(s) or situation(s) are coincidental. Please see the end of this chapter for important disclosure information regarding the financial products discussed.

Case Study #1: Finishing Medical School and Beginning PGY1 Year

Kelli is single and finishing up medical school. She will graduate in the spring and do a three year emergency medicine residency.

She has a few financial goals at this time, including:

- Develop a budget to manage the new residency salary
- Understand and sign up for appropriate employee benefits
- Consider purchasing a home or condo
- Understand and manage her student loan debt
- Have a plan for emergencies and unexpected events

The Numbers

Kelli will be living on $52,000/year or approximately $3,150/month take home. Even though her parents offered to loan her money for a down payment on a condo, she decided to rent an apartment because she will only be in the town for three years before moving somewhere else to continue her career.

Her Net Worth Statement

Fixed Assets:
    Savings Account: $3,000
    Checking Account: $1,000
    Money Market Account: $0
    Total Fixed Assets: **$4,000**

Variable Assets:
    Roth IRA: $0
    Mutual Funds: $0
    403b balance: $0
    Total Variable Assets: **$0**

Personal and Other Assets:
    Vehicle: $2,500
    Personal Property: $3,000
    Total: **$5,500**

Total Assets: **$9,500**

Liabilities:
    Credit Cards (21%): $2,300
    Student Loans (6.8%): $110,000
    Total Liabilities: **$112,300**

Net Worth (Assets Minus Liabilities):   **($102,800)**

The Financial Plan

Security and Confidence Stage:

- Set up a money market mutual fund to use as her emergency reserve instead of the savings account.
- Immediately begin aggressively paying off the credit card debt with most of her extra monthly surplus cash flow.
- Secure a private individual disability policy to insure her greatest asset: her ability to earn an income. This policy should protect her in her "own occupation", include a cost of living feature, and the maximum future purchase option allowing her to increase the coverage later without medical underwriting.
- Depending on cash flow, consider a repayment schedule for student loans using the income based repayment (IBR) rules. She should try to pay at least $2,500 of interest per year as that would be income tax deductible.
- Secure an inexpensive term life insurance policy with conversion features.

Capital Accumulation Stage:

- She should also start a monthly savings program that includes putting money into a mutual fund and a Roth IRA. The main objective here is just to get started and learning how to track these accounts on line increasing her knowledge and confidence level.

Tax-Advantaged Stage:

- Since she is at the lowest income (and tax bracket) for her career, and there is no employer match on the 403b account, she should wait to contribute to a pre-tax retirement account.

Speculation Stage:

- Wait until the rest of the pyramid is more established.

Case Studies

Summary

Kelli is normally a saver. She looks forward to beginning her training so she can start earning an income, which will allow her to pay off her credit cards and begin building a savings and investment plan. She is happy that she has started educating herself, building the base of her financial plan, and developing a trusting relationship with a financial planner.

Case Study #2: Second Year of Residency

Circumstances: Rupa is in her second year of Ob/Gyn residency. Her husband Rakesh just finished graduate school and landed his first full time job as a software engineer. They have no children.

Their financial goals and concerns are as follows:

- Pay off debt.
- Accumulate savings.
- Buy a starter home.
- Start a family.
- Begin retirement savings.
- Protect themselves against loss.

The Numbers

Rupa's income is $52,500 per year. Rakesh earns $65,000. They have $155,000 in student loans currently deferred at 3 percent interest. They have $3,000 in credit card debt and $4,000 in savings and few other assets and debts. Their take-home pay is $7,000 per month, and they currently have about $3,000 per month in discretionary income. Their current rent payment is $1,300 per month.

Case Studies

Their Net Worth Statement

Fixed Assets:
    Savings Account: $4,000
    Checking Account: $2,000
    Total Fixed Assets: **$6,000**

Variable Assets:
    Roth IRAs: $3,000
    403(b) Balance: $4,100
    Total Variable Assets: **$7,100**

Personal and Other Assets:
    Vehicles: $10,000
    Personal Property: $11,000
    Total: **$21,000**

Total Assets: **$34,100**

Liabilities:
    Vehicle Loan (7%): $10,000
    Credit Cards (18%): $3,000
    Student Loans (6.8%): $155,000
    Total Liabilities: **$168,000**

Net Worth (Assets minus Liabilities): **($133,900)**

The Financial Plan

Security and Confidence Stage:

- Apply the majority of the surplus dollars towards eliminating the credit card debt, and once paid off, into a money market mutual fund for emergencies as well as a home down payment fund.
- Apply for a forbearance for Rupa's student loans. Pay $2,500/year of interest to maximize the tax deduction since their income is less than $120,000.
- Obtain a private own occupation disability insurance policy for Rupa with the maximum future purchase option.
- Obtain inexpensive convertible term life insurance for both Rupa and Rakesh.
- Have a will drafted including health care directives.
- Increase emergency reserve fund once the credit cards are paid off.
- Purchase a $1 million umbrella liability policy if/when a home is purchased.

Capital Accumulation Stage:

- Survey the real estate market for affordability and start looking into areas of the city to purchase a home. Since they will most likely stay in the area when Rupa finishes residency, they would like to get a small starter home or condo taking advantage of the "buyers" market and low interest rates.
- Determine the equivalent mortgage payment to current rent payment. Due to the deductibility of mortgage interest and property taxes, it can be a large difference. In their case, the equivalent mortgage payment is $1,500, which would buy roughly a $250,000 home including taxes if financed at 4.5 percent and amortized over thirty years.
- Purchase a home or condo for around $250,000 if suitable housing can be found in that price range.

Case Studies

Tax-Advantaged Stage:

- Begin Roth IRA contributions once the credit cards are paid off and an emergency reserve has been established.
- Contribute 6 percent of Rakesh's income to his 401k to take full advantage of the 3 percent employer match.

Summary

The plan addresses current as well as future issues. The emphasis is placed on the *Security and Confidence Stage* by eliminating the credit cards, building an emergency fund, locking in life and disability insurance, and addressing their housing situation. Since the cost is relatively small, the future income has been protected with the addition of the properly structured disability policy that allows Rupa to add coverage when she enters private practice. The term life insurance policy guarantees life insurance coverage will be in place when Rupa and Rakesh start a family. The umbrella liability policy is their first asset protection component to better protect their personal assets from liability. The Roth IRA and 403(b) serve as building blocks to their investing and retirement needs.

Case Study # 3: Finishing Residency and Heading into Fellowship

Circumstances: George is in the final year of his orthopedic surgery residency and preparing for fellowship in a different state. He is single but expects to be married in 1-2 years with children to follow soon after. George owns a small home that he purchased at the beginning of his residency, which he is selling. He plans to rent during fellowship. Other than his mortgage, George has no other debt. His parents paid for his undergraduate and medical school. George has contributed the maximum annual contribution to his Roth IRA since he started residency and maintains a high balance in his checking account.

George's financial goals and concerns are as follows:

- invest the profit from sale of home
- get married and start a family in two years
- protect himself for future catastrophies

The Numbers:

George's current salary is $55,000 per year; however, in two moths his salary will be $57,000. His take home pay in two months will be $3,475 per month and after expenses are paid, he should have $1,000 per month of surplus cash flow available.

Case Studies

His Net Worth Statement:

Fixed Assets:
    Checking Account $11,000
    Total Fixed Assets: **$11,000**

Variable Assets:
    Roth IRA $22,000
    403(b) $6,500
    Total Variable Assets: **$28,500**

Personal and Other Assets:
    Home $142,000
    Vehicle $5,000
    Personal Property $2,000
    Total: **$149,000**

Total Assets: **$188,500**

Liabilities:
    Mortgage (5.25%) $129,000
    Total Liabilities: **$129,000**

Net Worth (Assets minus Liabilities)   **$59,500**

The Financial Plan:

Security and Confidence Stage:

- Maintain emergency fund such as savings account, interest bearing checking account or money market for funds currently held in non-interest bearing checking account. The balance of the cash flow surplus, after acquiring the necessary insurance programs noted below, should be committed to the same account for future expenses such as additional down payment on next home, wedding, etc.
- Obtain two individual disability policies with maximum future purchase option. Because each company limits his total future coverage, obtaining two separate policies with two separate companies allows George to protect himself to the fullest extent as he anticipates an income as a hand surgeon of over $500,000/year a few years into private practice.
- Obtain inexpensive convertible term life insurance.
- Purchase a $1 million liability umbrella policy.
- If he has a hard time selling his home, consider renting to an incoming resident in his department and refinancing to a lower interest rate.

Capital Accumulation Stage:

- Upon the sale of home, deposit proceeds in a secure interest-bearing account, such as a savings account, CD or money market. Funds will then be readily available to use for down payment on home purchase in 14 months.

Tax Advantaged Stage:

- Continue maximum Roth IRA contributions in current year, and in the subsequent year, if the combined income from a partial year fellowship and partial year in practice does not exceed the IRS income limits.

- Transfer the current Roth IRA to a fee based account using no load or load waived mutual funds instead of the bank money market where it is currently invested. Since this is long term money, the underlying investments should be more growth oriented using stocks and stock mutual funds.

Speculation Stage:

- Wait until the base of the financial pyramid is more established.

Summary:

At this stage of his career, the plan focuses on the importance of the Security and Confidence stage, strengthening the foundation or base to the pyramid. Emphasis is placed on building a solid foundation for the future by maintaining sufficient liquidity for future expenses and obtaining individual life and disability insurance to protect him and his future family's income. With minimal cost, George has protected current and future income through the purchase of an occupation specific disability policy with a future purchase option rider that allows him to add significant coverage once he is in practice without providing evidence of insurability. The term life insurance he acquires when he is insurable will provide immediate protection for when he starts a family. The liability umbrella is a foundational asset protection component. The Roth IRA and 403(b) are fundamental to their retirement needs.

Case Study # 4: Dual Physician Couple Five Years into Practice

Adam finished his plastic surgery residency five years ago and has been working hard to pay off debt and get established in his practice, while balancing time with his family. He was recently given the opportunity to buy into the practice and plans on this happening in the next month or two. His wife Natalie, a radiation oncologist, has been home part-time with their child for the last four and a half years. The plan is for her to work full-time when their son, Evan, starts kindergarten in the fall.

They have many financial goals at this time, including:

- Build "the house of their dreams" in a few years.
- Buy into Adam's practice and become a partner.
- Continue to pay off their debts.
- Start to save for Evan's college.
- Save for retirement.
- Reduce tax liability.
- Establish wealth/asset protection.
- Have a plan for emergencies and unexpected events.

The Numbers

Adam works in a midsized clinic as a plastic surgeon with an annual income of $350,000. Once he becomes partner, his annual income will increase to at least $600,000–700,000. He has to pay for his own benefits such as health insurance, disability insurance, life and malpractice insurance, as well as his own retirement plan. His disability policy is adequate for his current income, but would be insufficient coverage for the income he would be stepping into as a partner. He recently purchased a $500,000 term life insurance policy to cover the cost of the mortgage in the event of his death.

Natalie works part time in a radiation oncology practice with an annual income of $150,000. Once she starts working full-time in the fall, her annual income will increase to $320,000. She also has to provide her own insurance coverage, but unlike Adam, her employer has a qualified retirement plan that allows her to defer up to $16,500 of her income per year. The only life and disability coverage she owns are the small policies she purchased during residency five years ago.

Case Studies

In the next four months, their monthly take-home pay will increase to $38,000, and their monthly expenses will increase to $20,000 (which includes the business loan repayment for Adam's buy-in), leaving $18,000 per month in excess funds with which to plan.

Their Net Worth Statement

Fixed Assets:
Savings Account:	$45,000
Checking Account:	$23,000
Certificate of Deposit:	$30,000
Total Fixed Assets:	**$98,000**

Variable Assets:
IRA:	$13,000
Roth IRA:	$9,000
Mutual Funds:	$249,000
Individual Stocks:	$42,000
Total Variable Assets:	**$313,000**

Personal and Other Assets:
Home:	$675,000
Vehicles:	$60,000
Personal Property:	$40,000
Medical Practice (assuming Troy buys in):	$1,000,000
Total:	**$1,775,000**

Total Assets: **$2,186,000**

Liabilities:
Mortgage (30-year at 6%):	$510,000
Home Equity Line (7%):	$25,000
Vehicle Loan (4%):	$40,000
Student Loans (3.5%):	$150,000
Medical Practice Loan (7%):	$1,000,000
Total Liabilities:	**$1,725,000**

Net Worth (Assets Minus Liabilities): **$461,000**

Case Studies

The Financial Plan

Security and Confidence Stage:

- Increase their umbrella liability insurance to $4 million.
- Maximize uninsured/underinsured auto coverage.
- Secure an additional personal disability policy on both Adam and Natalie to supplement their current policies, which are inadequate for their income-to-be.
- Secure $5 million of life insurance on Adam and $3 million on Natalie using a combination of over-funded variable adjustable policies and term insurance.
- Increase the home equity line of credit to be used for emergencies.*
- Stretch out student loans and home mortgage as long as possible, taking advantage of the low interest rates.
- Draft wills, trusts, and appropriate estate planning documents.*

* Find a qualified attorney to draft documents, and make sure you understand all terms and conditions of any arrangements. Financial Advisors do not provide tax or legal advice

Capital Accumulation Stage:

- Commit to saving at least $15,000 per month into the following:
- Initiate 529 Plan for Evan's college and fund $1,000 per month.
- Initiate a brokerage account and build a portfolio of non-qualified mutual funds ($7,000 per month).
- Fund variable adjustable life policies up to the limits allowed, that do not turn the policies into modified endowment contracts (MEC's) at $7,000 per month. Not only do these policies have some tax advantages, but Adam and Natalie worked with their attorney and learned the policies are also exempt from creditors in their state which provides them some very significant asset protection.
- Consider building their dream house sooner rather than later, to take advantage of today's lower interest rates, and to allow enjoyment of the house with the family for many more years.

Tax-Advantaged Stage:

- Adam and his partners contribute $49,000 into a self directed retirement account. They each have a fee based account using load waived mutual funds. Adam chose an aggressive growth portfolio that is broadly diversified across all sectors and will monitor this quarterly with his financial advisors.
- Continue to maximize the contribution into Natalie's 401k retirement plan ($16,500 per year); making sure this is actively managed using a carefully constructed growth-style portfolio.

Speculation Stage:

- They are not comfortable using any of their funds for speculative investing at this time, and have decided to continue to build the "base" of the pyramid as described earlier. At some point, they would like to pursue some riskier investments, which would fit into this stage.

Summary

With newly added risk management vehicles such as the increased life, disability, and umbrella liability insurances, their new plan is firmly anchored. Adam and Natalie are happy knowing their estate plan is in good order and able to adapt as their family and financial plan grows. In addition, they are now able to adapt to their increasing income by properly allocating their short-, mid-, and long-term savings. And lastly, they have started to work with an architect to build their dream home, and can pursue that sooner than they imagined. They can't believe how fast all of these changes have taken place, but are relieved to have an efficient plan that is able to keep up with their very busy lives.

Case Study #5: Mid Career Job Change

Anne and Tom are both in their mid forties and have three children, ages sixteen, fifteen, and eleven. Anne has worked as a pediatrician at a large teaching hospital since finishing her residency from the same institution. Tom is beginning to get back into consulting but still finds himself quite busy running the household, taking care of all the finances, and attending all the various activities the kids are in. He's figuring that any income will be offset by his expenses but as the kids get older and into college; he will be able to build up his business with the goal of making enough money to cover some of the kids' college expenses.

Recently, Anne has been approached by a fast growing multi-specialty group that is competing with the teaching hospital. She has been offered a significant signing bonus, a very competitive benefit package, and a three year income guarantee. She is torn between her loyalty to her existing partners, and patients, with the opportunity of increasing her income significantly while working a more manageable schedule. She has become increasingly disappointed with the current teaching hospital and all the "politics" stating that "I just want to practice medicine."

Their primary financial goals include:

- Anne taking a more active role in the financial planning process.
- Determining what amount needs to be saved for each child in order to pay for 75% of college tuition and related expenses.
- Reviewing life and disability insurance for both of them.
- Analyze their current retirement which includes a defined benefit pension and a money purchase pension with the ability to contribute to a 403b, and 457 deferred compensation plan, to the retirement package being offered through the recruiting employer.
- Determine if their investment mix is in line with their investment objectives and risk tolerance, and if the amount they are saving for retirement is sufficient.
- Maintaining a greater amount of cash surplus available for planned and unanticipated expenses like family vacations, auto purchases and repairs, home improvements, etc.

The Numbers

Anne's current annual income is $155,000 where the offer from the new employer is guaranteed at $185,000, plus a signing bonus to be negotiated. While not guaranteed forever, she believes that the new clinic is dedicated to growing and while she would miss the responsibilities of teaching younger residents, it is hard to pass up $30,000/year of increased income.

The financial plan focused on reviewing all the insurance and retirement plans being offered through the current and potential new employer. An emphasis was on comparing the complex retirement options through both employers. While different in structure, the new employer offers a substantial match and a contribution to each physician's retirement account to make up for the fact that the teaching hospital has a defined benefit pension contribution that Anne would be walking away from.

Case Studies

Net Worth Statement

Fixed Assets:
    Savings Account): $4,500
    Checking Account: $2,200
    Money Market Account: $8,800
    Total Fixed Assets: **$15,500**

Variable Assets:
    Non-Qualified Jointly Held Brokerage Account: $58,000
    Individual Stocks: $29,000
    Anne's Retirement Plan from Former Employer: $287,000
    Tom's 401k and IRA Rollover: $218,000
    Total Variable Assets: **$592,000**

Personal and Other Assets:
    Home: $850,000
    Vehicles: $52,000
    Personal Property: $38,000
    Total: **$940,000**

Total Assets: **$1,547,500**

Liabilities:
    Mortgage (30 year at 6%): $580,000
    Vehicle Loan: $24,000
    Credit Card: $600
    Total Liabilities: **$604,600**

Net Worth (Assets Minus Liabilities):   **$942,900**

The Financial Plan

Security and Confidence Stage:

- We suggested that they take the majority of the signing bonus and split between a money market mutual fund and a very conservative mutual fund to increase their emergency reserves to a more appropriate level.
- They should also refinance their mortgage to a new thirty year fixed rate at 4%. They could do a fifteen year mortgage, but would rather stretch the mortgage out so they can put more money towards the kids' college education funds. The 2% savings on their $580,000 mortgage will save over $11,000/year of interest.
- In reviewing the life and disability insurance, Anne owns a $1,000,000 twenty-year term policy that was purchased fifteen years ago. In addition, there is almost $600,000 of group life insurance at the current employer. Anne also owns a disability policy with a $3,000 monthly benefit. The only life insurance on Tom is the spousal benefit of $50,000 through Anne's employer. After a "needs analysis' which quantifies the amount of coverage someone needs, Anne should have $2,200,000 of coverage and Tom should have $500,000.
- We recommend that Anne increase her personal insurance to $2,000,000 supplementing this with another $200,000 through work. This life insurance protection should be made up of a combination of permanent and term insurance. The use of the term policy will also allow us to stretch the amount of insurance given the dollars we are allocating from their cash flow, and the permanent plan will provide a vehicle to accumulate cash value on a tax-deferred basis. The cash value can be used at a later point to supplement retirement income. Tom currently does not own life insurance, but should own at least $500,000 of coverage. In the event or his premature death, Anne would be able to work on a 60% schedule to spend more time with the kids during these teenage years.

Case Studies

Capital Accumulation Stage:

- In addition to saving for retirement, they will be adding the earmarked college education mutual fund to the brokerage account. Additional contributions will be used to build capital for future major expenditures such as a possible vacation home, remodeling project, and other larger financial expenses for the children.
- Along with the supplemental retirement savings and additional education funding contributions going into the non-qualified brokerage account, Tom and Caroline should transfer the stocks to their existing brokerage account.
- Because they hope to fund 75 % of their children's college expenses, a total of $1,200 monthly will be invested into a 529 Plan for each of the three children, and the remaining 40 % or $600 a month will be invested into one mutual fund the parents will own. Tom and Anne assumed the college expenses would be in the $30,000 range, which we assumed would increase at a rate of 5% a year.

Tax Advantaged Stage

- We advise Anne to roll over her retirement plan into an IRA. We recommend she use a brokerage account. When deciding what allocation is appropriate for her account, we also need to consider the investment choices within the new retirement plans so all of these long term dollars work together.
- After reviewing the retirement analysis, it was determined that in addition to Anne contributing the maximum to the 401k plan, they should also be saving monthly. An automatic monthly savings plan will be established that will be invested into Tom and Caroline's non-qualified brokerage account.

Summary

Anne and Tom are now on a path toward accomplishing their financial goals; college for their children and their own retirement while doing an excellent job of managing their year-to-year expenditures. They are taking advantage of tax-preferred items such as 529 Plans, the 401k plan, and cash value life insurance policies. In the event of a death, disability, or illness, they have properly protected their family financially. The investment plan will allow them to build for future expenses, and the cash account in the money market should provide them with funds to do the things they enjoy doing with their family, without the need to go into debt or create a problem when unexpected expenses occur. They enjoy having better control of her investment choices with her IRA rollover versus having the funds at her prior employer's 401k. She also finds working more enjoyable knowing that "there is a light at the end of the tunnel", and her hard work is helping them achieve their financial goals. They will continue to meet with their financial advisor to monitor this financial and life plan together.

Case Studies

Variable life insurance and mutual funds are sold only by prospectus. The prospectus contains important information about the product's investment objectives, charges and expenses, as well as the risks and other information associated with the product. You may obtain a copy of the prospectus from your representative. You should carefully consider the risks and investment charges of a specific product before investing. You should always read the prospectus carefully before investing. Investments in a money market fund are neither insured nor guaranteed by the FDIC, or any government agency. Although the fund seeks to preserve the value of your investment at $1.00 per share, it is possible to lose money by investing in the fund.

Life insurance products contain fees, such as mortality and expense charges, and may contain restrictions, such as surrender charges. Policy loans and withdrawals may create an adverse tax result in the event of a lapse or policy surrender, and will reduce both the cash value and death benefit. If a policy is over funded and becomes a modified endowment contract (MEC), the contract's earnings will be taxed as ordinary income at withdrawal, and may be subject to a 10% penalty if withdrawn before age 59 1/2. Please keep in mind that the primary reason to purchase a life insurance product is the death benefit.

A 529 college savings plan is a tax-advantaged investment program designed to help pay for qualified higher education costs. Participation in a 529 plan does not guarantee that the contributions and investment returns will be adequate to cover higher education expenses. Contributors to the plan assume all investment risk, including the potential for loss of principal, and any penalties for non-educational withdrawals. Your state of residence may offer state tax advantages to residents who participate in the in-state plan, subject to meeting certain conditions or requirements. You may miss out on certain state tax advantages should you choose another state's 529 plan. Any state based benefits should be one of many appropriately weighted factors to be considered in making an investment decision. You should consult with your financial, tax or other advisor to learn more about how state based benefits (including any limitations) would apply to your specific circumstances. You may also wish to contact your home state's 529 plan Program Administrator to learn more about the benefits that might be available to you by investing in the in-state plan.

Appendix A

Employee Benefits Checklist

for the

Physician

✓   1. Salary Structure
         Year 1: _____
         Year 2: _____
         Year 3: _____
         Year 4: _____
         Year 5: _____

✓   2. Major Medical Insurance Benefits
         A.   Deductible _____
         B.   Top limits _____
         C.   Hospitalization benefits for self and family
               (describe) _____
               _____

         D.   Medical and dental reimbursement programs
               1.   Top limit _____

✓   3. Group Long-Term Disability Insurance Benefits
         A.   Amount   _____
         B.   Premiums paid by
               Self: _____
               Corporation: _____
         C.   Wage continuation program if disabled
               (describe) _____
               _____

         D. Short-term disability insurance (describe) _____
         _____

✓   4. Group Life Insurance Benefits
         A.   Face amount while in practice _____
         B.   Face amount after retirement _____

✓   5. Pension/Profit Sharing Plan Benefits
         A.   What are the eligibility requirements?
         _____

         B.   Where are the funds invested?
         _____

Appendix A

      C. What is the formula?

      D. What is the vesting schedule?

      E. What does the most recent actuarial valuation show past service liability to be?

      F. What is the availability of voluntary contribution under the plan?

✓   6. Malpractice Insurance
      A. Who pays the premiums?

      B. Umbrella coverage

      C. Amount of coverage

      D. Claims made or occurrence policy

✓   7. Automobile Reimbursement
      A. Auto
      B. Repairs
      C. Gas

✓   8. Vacation Policy
      A. How are vacation times determined

      B. Amount of vacation time available

      C. Compensation arrangements if more time is taken

✓   9. Reimbursement for Continuing Education

    A. Reimbursement for attendance at conferences

    B. Reimbursement for professional affiliation dues/subscriptions

    C. Reimbursement for time off used to prepare for Boards _____

✓   10. Does the firm arrange for a line of credit for the new physician?

✓   11. Are there any privileges restricted to senior physicians?

✓   12. Are there any extra duties expected of the new physician that are not performed by senior physicians?
    A. Evening calls _____
    B. Weekend calls _____
    C. Other _____

✓   13. Is the new physician invited to all corporation meetings and discussions with professional advisors?
    A. At the time he/she joins the practice?

    B. When he/she becomes a stockholder?

✓   14. Procedure by which a new physician becomes a stockholder?
    A. Waiting time

    B. Terms of the purchase

    C. Assets included

D. At what point an equal stockholder
_____

✓ 15. Does the practice own its own building? _____

✓ 16. Are there provisions for the new physician to buy into the building?
    A. Share of interest _____
    B. Terms of buy-in _____

✓ 17. How are accounts receivable handled?
    A. In buying in _____
    B. Paying off an existing stockholder _____

✓ 18. How are termination benefits handled?
    A. Stock interest _____
    B. Receivables _____

✓ 19. Does the firm have a relationship with:
    Please clarify the relationship.
    A. Banker? _____

    B. Insurance Agent? _____

    C. Financial Planner? _____

    D. Realtor? _____

    E. Stockbroker? _____

✓ 20. Does the firm's attorney handle estate planning for the new physician? _____ Who pays the fee? _____

✓ 21. Does the firm's accountant handle tax returns for the new physician? _____ Who pays the fee? _____

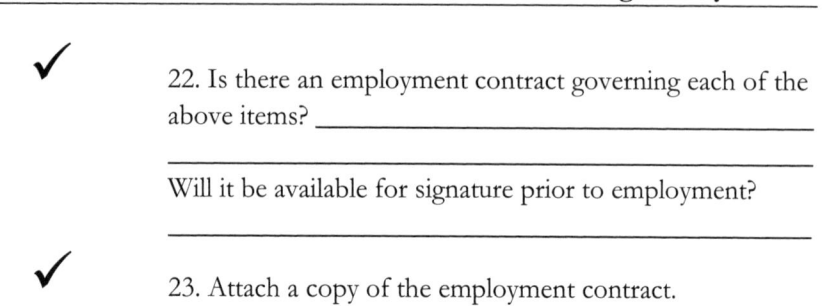

✓   22. Is there an employment contract governing each of the above items? _____

Will it be available for signature prior to employment? _____

✓   23. Attach a copy of the employment contract.

ABOUT THE AUTHORS

Todd D. Bramson, CFP®, ChFC, CLU

Certified Financial Planner™ practitioner Todd D. Bramson has been working in the field of financial planning for over twenty-six years, and has been recognized as one of the 150 best financial advisors for doctors nationwide by *Medical Economics* magazine. He is one of only a few financial advisors who have been listed each of the last seven times *Medical Economics* has provided this survey. Additionally, Todd is an Editorial Consultant with the magazine.

An exceptional teacher, as well as a motivating author and speaker, he has been quoted in numerous financial publications, and has spent several years as the financial expert on the local NBC live 5:00 p.m. news broadcast. In June of 2004, he spoke at the prestigious Million Dollar Round Table, a worldwide organization of the top five percent of all financial services professionals. He is also the author and creator of the *Real Life Financial Planning* book series.

Mr. Bramson's belief, "If the trust is there, the miles don't matter," has earned him devoted clients not only in his hometown of Madison, Wisconsin, but in most states throughout the country. Along with all the designations expected of a trusted financial professional, he is committed to keeping abreast of all the developments in his field, and to playing an active role in his community. He conducts regular seminars and is active in his community, including the Breakfast Optimist Club, The Evans Scholars Alumni Foundation, Blackhawk Country Club, and a director with Western Golf Association.

Todd is also the founder and president of Bramson and Associates LLC. Information on his company, philosophy, and services can be found at www.toddbramson.com. You will quickly see that Todd is dedicated to providing valuable wisdom through his books, web site, presentations, and newsletters.

Jon C. Ylinen

Jon C. Ylinen is a Financial Advisor with North Star Resource Group. Jon maintains a national practice with his main office in located in Madison, Wisconsin. Frequently, he travels throughout the country conducting seminars and workshops. He joined North Star Resource Group in 2007 and is a Partner of North Star's Medical Division, a group of advisors who specialize in working with physicians, dentists and pharmacists, sharing best practices and the latest trends. In his first full year at North Star, he earned the "New Associate of the Year" honor. In addition, Jon has written for numerous financial publications including a regular column for *Physician's Money Digest* and *Medical Economics*. He has a degree in Personal Finance from the University of Wisconsin.

Jon's financial planning practice caters almost exclusively to physicians. He works with medical students, residents, fellows, and in practice and staff physicians. He and Todd Bramson have a joint practice that specializes in comprehensive financial planning with specific strategies to the unique financial circumstances that medical professionals face, including debt management, risk management, asset protection planning, investment planning, retirement planning, tax planning and estate planning. Jon and Todd have a national practice comprised of hundreds of clients throughout the United States. They continue to grow through referrals from existing clients.

Jon enjoys spending time with family and friends, traveling, working out and crossing things off his "Sports Bucket List". Ask him about this and have some fun discussing some very interesting and fun short and long term goals for enjoying life, family, friends, and sports.

Robert Kaufer

Robert Kaufer has been practicing law for 17 years in the areas of estate planning, asset protection, physician contract review and various other business law matters. Prior to becoming an attorney he was a high school teacher and college baseball coach.

He received his bachelor's degree in education from the University of Wisconsin at River falls, his Juris Doctorate (JD) from the University of Hamline School of law and a Master of Business Administration (MBA) from the University of St. Thomas.

Robert is licensed to practice law and maintains a presence in Minnesota, Wisconsin and Arizona and currently resides in Saint Paul, Minnesota with his wife Stephanie and daughters Mickelle and Mackenna. His legal philosophy is to educate the client about their options and then help them make the best choices to meet their unique goals and objectives. Mr. Kaufer is not affiliated with CRI Securities or Securian Financial Services Inc.

To contact Robert Kaufer:

Phone: 1-888-711-4524
Web site: www.robertkaufer.com
E-mail: Robert@robertkaufer.com

NORTH STAR RESOURCE GROUP

Todd D. Bramson, CFP®, ChFC, CLU
North Star Resource Group
2945 Triverton Pike Drive #200
Madison, WI 53711
Direct: 1-608-271-3669 ext. 218
todd.bramson@northstarfinancial.com

Jon C. Ylinen
North Star Resource Group
2945 Triverton Pike Drive #200
Madison, WI 53711
Direct: 1-608-271-3669 ext. 299
jon@northstarfinancial.com

Variable life insurance, variable annuities, and mutual funds are sold only by prospectus. The prospectus contains important information about the product's investment objectives, charges and expenses, as well as the risks and other information associated with the product. You may obtain a copy of the prospectus from your representative. You should carefully consider the risks and investment charges of a specific product before investing. You should always read the prospectus carefully before investing.

This book contains a lot of information and investment/planning strategies. Keeping in mind that everyone's financial situation is different, the strategies and concepts discussed within this book may not be appropriate for everyone. You should meet with your financial, legal, and tax advisors before implementing any financial, legal, or tax strategy.

The tax concepts that are addressed in this book are current as of 2011. Tax laws change frequently, and any tax concept addressed in this book may not be applicable after 2011.

Todd D. Bramson and Jon C. Ylinen are registered representatives and investment advisor representatives with CRI Securities LLC and Securian Financial Services Inc., members of FINRA/SIPC, registered investment advisors. CRI Securities LLC is affiliated with Securian Financial Services Inc. and North and North Star Resource Group. Securian Financial Services, Inc. and North Star Resource Group are not affiliated. They do not provide specific tax or legal advice. Please consult a tax and/or legal professional before implementing any strategy.

Separate from the financial plan and our role as financial planner, we may recommend the purchase of specific investment or insurance products or accounts. These product recommendations are not part of the financial plan and you are under no obligation to follow them.

TRN: 413744
DOFU: 2-2012

ASPATORE